The future favors those leaders who effectively engage upcoming generations. Leaders leverage change for strategic advantage! *Millennial Matters* is a timely, provocative resource to help any manager play offense in this high potential generational transition. God has seeded this generation with eternal potential. Will you unleash it?

—Mike Sharrow, President & CEO,
The C12 Group, LLC

In *Millennials Matter*, Danita Bye has identified the importance of equipping the millennial generation to succeed owners transitioning out of their businesses. In this historically largest ever transfer of generational wealth, Danita's focus is to mentor, coach, and mobilize the millennial generation to lead companies to even greater levels, while at the same time preserving the legacy of the business owner.

—Rob Gales, Managing Director, VERCOR

Millennials Matter is a practical culmination of Danita Bye's life and leadership journey both professionally and personally as she has purposed to be a student of millennials stepping into the workforce as young professionals. You'll enjoy Danita's well written and researched book as a practical tool for navigating the perils of successfully onboarding millennials into your enterprise.

—Pete Henschel, Cru, National Field Director;
Executive Director, Executive and Entrepreneurial Leadership Forum; Executive Director, Global Leadership Forum

While reading Danita's book, I found myself frequently introspecting and reminiscing. How am I a typical millennial? How can I overcome my millennial weaknesses? How can I leverage my millennial strengths? *Millennial Matters* helped me realize obvious mistakes I had made while managing millennials and bolstered my ability to lead my peers and more importantly, myself.

—Cooper Buss, millennial Entrepreneur, Life Acoustics;
Director of Customer Success-Digital Marketing
ResortsAndLodges.com

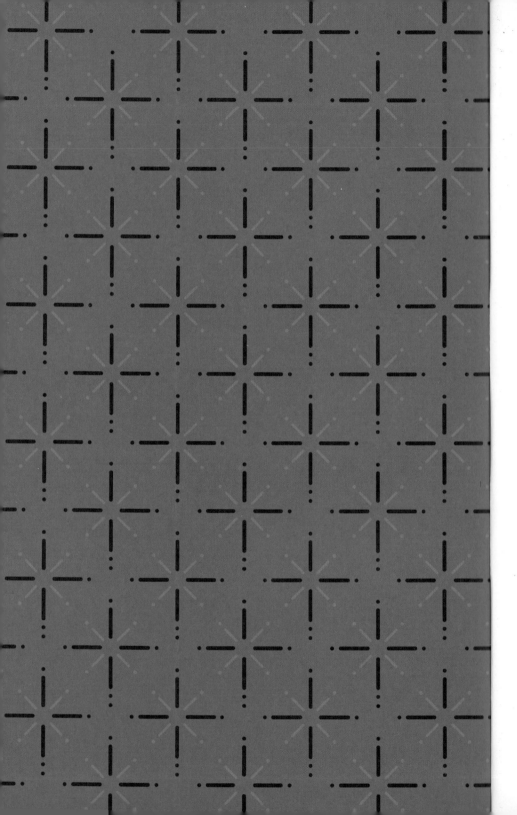

Millenials Matter is packed with tips for connecting with, mentoring, and developing the leaders of the future. I know from experience that for seasoned leaders, there is no greater joy than mentoring a first-time manager. Why? Because mentor and mentee learn so much from each other in the process! Danita Bye has written a fabulous guidebook for leaders in every generation. Read it and make a connection!

—KEN BLANCHARD, coauthor of *The New One Minute Manager*® and *Lead Like Jesus Revisited*

Timely and on point, *Millennials Matter* is filled with truths you and your team can act on to make a difference in your future and our future. Inspiring, relevant, and actionable, this book is a tool box to build trust and influence, and impact our current and future leaders. We need to do this now!

—DAVID HORSAGER, Trust Edge Leadership Institute

Danita Bye's passion to see the next generation realize their God-given potential comes through in *Millennials Matter*. This timely and engaging book equips leaders to better understand and effectively invest in millennials. It should be on the reading list of every CEO, supervisor, teacher, pastor, coach, counselor, parent, and more.

—HAL DONALDSON, President, Convoy of Hope
Author, *Your Next 24 Hours: One Day of Kindness Can Change Everything*

Millennials Matter is a must read for anyone interested in preparing new leaders to meet the challenges of the future. Danita leads us through the steps to help develop values-based difference in emerging adults and gives us the tools to discover the potential in others to lead. Reading this book will compel you to evaluate your responsibility to transfer your leadership attributes to those who follow.

—ED SCHAFER, Governor of North Dakota (1992–2000)
US Secretary of Agriculture (2008–2009)

Millennials Matter is a must read for anyone wanting to unlock the next talent rich generation for organization and business success. Danita is totally dialed into this generation's brilliance and unique aptitudes while possessing keen insight into what to do with their seeming collective shortcomings. Her clear and straightforward strategies will rescue you from old patterns and jumpstart you into a fresh, relevant model yielding unparalleled outcomes. Clear your schedule today to read *Millennials Matter*, and you will change lives. Yours may be one of them.

—KAREN A. BERG-JOHNSON, Director of Leadership Giving, PULSE, a millennial-engaged Christian nonprofit

The why is never-changing. Leadership is fluid. Just about the time leaders are in that sweet spot where wisdom meets humble confidence, it's time to begin passing the torch. Effectively making this transition has long-term ramifications. The how has to be ever-changing too. The twenty-first century's new wave of leaders, millennials, require an entirely new understanding by leaders that started in the twentieth century. Leaders involved with CBMC have a desire to mentor and disciple millennials but aren't exactly sure how. Danita provides a powerful toolkit to guide leaders who desire to transition well and bear fruit that lasts.

—ALAN SMITH, Area Executive Director, CBMC Northland

Millennial Matters is a must read on the up-and-coming, new world talent. This book's counsel can maximize your company, mobilize your leaders, and realize your legacy! Danita Bye's insightful research and passion to help equip and coach business leaders on next-gen character based leaders is stunningly captured in *Millennial Matters*!

—DEBORAH YUNGNER, CEO-Visioneer, ERBUS Inc.; Vice President, BizDev; CoCreateX; recipient of the Woman Inventor of the Year, USA

Millennials Matter is a great resource to help implement the three recommendations I give to CPAs developing millennials: thanking them once a week for something specific they have done; getting them the resources they need from their perspective (i.e., don't micro-manage them); and giving them a chance to shine.

—MICHAEL GREGORY, Chief Manager, Michael Gregory Consulting, LLC; Author, *Peaceful Resolutions* and *The Servant Manager*

As an educator in both secondary and higher education and now a university administrator, *Millennials Matter* reinforces my belief that virtue is the answer for a world crying for meaning, but more importantly, gives guidance on how to lead what could be the greatest generation yet. Thank you, Danita, for this pay-it-forward insight!

—JEROME J. RICHTER, Vice President for Public Affairs, University of Mary

Danita Bye is a great listener. There is no possible way to solve the puzzle of millennials without understanding how they think, and that only comes through listening. This book is your road map for listening to and building them into great leaders.

—SCOTT HENNEN, Host, *What's On Your Mind* radio show; Partner, Flag Family Media

Danita Bye's thorough understanding of the critical business issue regarding the development of millennials and her unique ability to address this topic is critical to your future success. Creating awareness, mobilizing efforts, and mapping out the right solution are required if you are to successfully overcome potential roadblocks. A "coach and mentor" for your millennials, I would highly recommend you reach out to Danita. Your legacy will be in good hands.

—PAUL BALUS, Senior Director of Global Sales and Corporate Training, Skyline Displays

Millennials
Matter

Leaders build leaders.
Keep building.
Danita Bye

DANITA BYE

BroadStreet
PUBLISHING

BroadStreet Publishing® Group, LLC
Racine, Wisconsin, USA
BroadStreetPublishing.com

Millennials **Matter:**
Proven Strategies for Building Your Next-Gen Leaders

ISBN-13: 978-1-4245-5558-1 (hardcover)
ISBN-13: 978-1-4245-5559-8 (e-book)

Stock or custom editions of BroadStreet Publishing titles may be purchased in bulk for educational, business, ministry, fundraising, or sales promotional use. For information, please e-mail info@broadstreetpublishing.com.

Cover design by Chris Garborg at garborgdesign.com
Interior design and typeset by Katherine Lloyd at theDESKonline.com

Printed in China

17 18 19 20 21 5 4 3 2 1

For my parents, Fred and Joyce Evans,
for stewarding their gifts of
encouragement and hospitality.

Contents

Section 1 - Strengthen Character

Part 1: Cultivate a Courageous Core

Part 2: Practice Proactive Self-Care

Section 2 - Lead with Confidence

Part 1: Model an Impact Mind-set

Part 2: Strengthen Your *Sisu* Spirit

Section 3 - Engage with Collaboration

Part 1: Respect Relationship Wiring

Part 2: Inspire the Investment Effect

⁘ Shifting Gears

Seemingly unrelated disconnected events happen over the course of life. Then one day you wake up and realize, *All those events were leading up to now.* It's the moment when God merges your years of talents, skills, experiences, and wisdom for a greater purpose.

A few years ago, I received an invitation to give the commencement speech for my alma mater, the University of Sioux Falls, in Sioux Falls, South Dakota. That was deeply meaningful and honoring, especially since the previous two speakers had been the governor of South Dakota and a senator from the state. I was excited and nervous.

My three children fell within the definition of *millennial*, but I wasn't sure I was in touch with their world. After all, my expertise was with business owners—collaborating with them to build high-performance sales teams that consistently and predictably grow revenues, raise margins, and take market share. I didn't have experience inspiring college students to be world changers, and these young people were stepping into the most severe global turmoil any generation has ever known. I set aside every nonessential task at work in order to pour myself into the message I would soon deliver to this graduating class of college students.

The commencement speech went even better than I'd imagined. It was an amazing experience. Long afterward, students and parents told me that my message had resonated with them, and I was pleased it had. When I returned home, I checked that item off my to-do list. Then I started tackling the next priority on my one-page strategic plan, relieved to be able to return to my sales consulting business.

This is often true of seasoned business leaders, isn't it? We volunteer to do an emerging-entrepreneur event or we go out to coffee with a friend's son who needs career advice, and we count it as "doing our part" to help the next generation. Then we resume our usual mode of leading our teams or running our businesses.

However, surprising events began to unfold for me. Just a few months after the commencement speech, Dr. Mark Benedetto, then president of the University of Sioux Falls, telephoned. My husband and I were living in Minneapolis at the time, and Mark said, "Danita, I'm going to be in Minneapolis. I would love to have dinner with you and see if you're interested in being on the board of trustees."

My more cynical self? It thought, *Oh, I know how these conversations go. We'll have a delicious dinner while we discuss general topics. Then we'll get to the dividing line in the conversation, that point at which he'll ask me, "How much money would you like to donate to the university?" And if the amount is big enough, then I'll get invited onto the board of trustees.*

But Mark's invitation came at an intriguing time. I had a growing interest in the impact higher education might have in nurturing young adults to be more prepared when they enter the workforce. What might higher education do to close the gap that business leaders were identifying in character, emotional maturity, interpersonal skills, and communication competences in our next generation of leaders?

So I decided to go and have the conversation.

Mark and I enjoyed a great dinner. Eventually we got to the dividing line, when he would start talking about money. Surprisingly, the conversation went in a different direction. He revealed that he was in a transition time of his presidency, that he was starting to consider leaders he might encourage to apply for the position when he retired. And my name was one of those that came to mind.

I was stunned. *My* name?

He talked a little more about his vision, then he said, "Danita, you're brilliant [his word, not mine] at encouraging the students to consider their impact in the world, at challenging them to be world changers, and at inspiring them to integrate their faith into everything they do. Plus, you interacted so well with the parents, the faculty, and all the stakeholders. You would be perfect!"

I came up with an immediate objection. "I'm in business, which operates ten times faster than academia. And not only that, I'm an entrepreneur. I operate ten times faster than business does. It is oil and water. It would never, never work."

Without blinking an eye, he answered, "Danita, that is exactly why I thought of you. Because that's what higher education needs."

Not being persuaded by his quick reply, I proceeded with six additional objections.

After every one, he said, "Yes, and that's the reason I thought of you for this position."

Later that night, as I walked out of the meeting, I dialed my husband to tell him about the crazy conversation I'd had.

He listened, then said, "Danita, this role would be perfect for you."

What? My husband is practical and realistic. He's the one who keeps my feet on the ground. I'd expected him to squash the idea.

But his response launched me into the next thirty days. Never in my wildest dreams had I considered such a role. During that time, all I could think and dream about was the incredible platform and opportunity to impact the next generation to be world changers—to be a catalyst in building young leaders of character who would then build other young leaders of character during their lifetime. I even rehearsed my acceptance speech.

Well, I know enough about myself to know that I can be excited for thirty days. The true test is what happens on day thirty-one. Sure enough, on day thirty-one I was back to normal.

That was on a Monday. But on Friday my son called me, and normal was about to shift gears on me.

My son had just attended the Willow Creek Global Leadership Conference and wanted to fill me in on what he'd heard from the various speakers. He relayed events in his upbeat, enthusiastic but somewhat disconnected way. Suddenly, in mid-sentence, he stopped: "Mom, I have a message for you." His voice shifted gears. It had gravitas, intent, and total focus: "Mom, you must prioritize the passing on of your leadership wisdom and insights to the next generation."

The words, coming from my twenty-three-year-old son, struck right to my core.

Then the serious moment ended. He returned to his typical happy-go-lucky self with, "Gotta go, Mom. Hanging out with some friends. Talk later."

In the days and weeks that followed, my son's words gained momentum in my thoughts and heart. I wondered why I was so deeply affected by our conversation, other than the fact that this "message" came from my young adult son and not a seasoned leadership guru or spiritual mentor. For him to break stride and be so intently focused was jaw-dropping in its rareness.

As I considered the commencement speech, the conversation with Mark about the board of trustees, and what my son had said, something awakened inside me. This "something" was new, vibrant. It carried a different sensation than I'd ever felt before. For me, this was the Holy Spirit saying, "I need you to pay attention to this, to shift your focus."

Soon after, early one autumn morning, I took my journaling session outside. Shorter days had arrived, and with them the chill that hung in the air. I settled down to do some serious reflecting on this sequence of events.

Mentoring millennials wasn't on any of my to-do lists. It wasn't part of my one-page strategic plan. It was nowhere on my radar screen. Yet I was being invited to zero in on the development of up-and-coming, character-based business and sales leaders. Why? So that they might become positive agents of change in our world. I was being called to shift gears and to positively impact their spiritual and leadership transformations.

That moment marked a two-wheeled turn in my direction.

During my subsequent reflection on the "leadership wisdom and insights" part of my son's message, I dove back into my 101-page spiritual and leadership development case study, "The Lady with the Lantern: Called to Love," which I'd compiled for Ministry Leadership 501 at Bethel University in 2006. One hundred and one pages—that's a long paper when it comes to examining your life! The analysis process had been based on one of my favorite leadership development books, *The Making of a Leader: Recognizing the Lessons and Stages of Leadership Development* written by Dr. Robert J. Clinton.

The final section of the case study asked me to identify key experiences or turning points in each leadership development stage, starting with when I was three years old. I answered the following questions:

- What leadership lesson did I learn through this experience?
- What wisdom did I gain?
- How did I respond differently in this experience than others might have reacted?
- What did I learn about God?
- How do these insights impact my relationship with God?
- How do these insights impact my responsibilities as a godly ambassador?

As you might imagine, several aha moments struck during this introspective exercise. One key discovery was that many of my leadership and spiritual formation lessons were rooted in my growing-up years in an eight-hundred-square-foot homestead shack on an isolated cattle ranch in northwestern North Dakota.

This realization ignited the need to blog, and I titled my first blog series "DAKOTA Leadership." Over time, that series evolved to become "Millennial Matters."

Why am I sharing this story?

During the many hours I've talked with trusted mentors, colleagues, family, and friends, one realization has stood out: millennials need us. The world is undergoing a rapid shift, and millions of young adults struggle to find their footing. Amid this cultural chaos, next-gen leaders need the benefit of what we know. They need our wisdom and our insights. This message is for all of us who are builders of companies and leaders of people.

What happened with the University of Sioux Falls offer? In the end, I discerned that being a university president was not for me. It would be oil and water. I also realized that my passion is for energizing and equipping business leaders to coach and mentor (dare we say, disciple) emerging leaders. The results of their investment in these leaders are threefold. They will:

- Maximize their business
- Mobilize their leaders
- Realize their legacy

Millennials:
A Lasting Plan to Realize Your Legacy

Leaders build leaders. Most of the experienced business owners I work with are focused on driving growth and performance. Yes, business results are important. However, many of these leaders also know that the legacy they leave, both at work and at home, matters even more. This is the mark of true wisdom and effective stewardship.

We live in the wealthiest nation during the wealthiest time in history. And some of us even live in the wealthiest state or suburb. In Luke 12:48, Jesus says that to whom much is given, much will be required. Let's be frank. We have been given much, haven't we? If you've traveled internationally, you know what we've been given goes beyond what we imagined when we were young, planning our careers, and crafting our life goals.

What do Jesus' words mean today?

I submit that mentoring the next generation of leaders, especially those that God has placed in our sphere of influence, is part of what is required of us. This is an unprecedented time in history. Millennials are entering a global economy that's filled with threats and opportunities beyond the imagination of any previous generation. Ethical issues abound with the advent of robotics, artificial intelligence, quantum mechanics, genetic engineering, and a multitude of other complexities. It's understandable that they're filled with mixed emotions (ranging from fear to excitement) about making a positive difference. The world is crazy. Our young leaders need our guidance; they need us to pass on the experience we have received and the wisdom we have gained. And, to maximize their influence in the global community, we need fresh insight into how God wants us to mentor and coach this generation.

Your legacy making doesn't end when you retire. In *The Making of a Leader: Recognizing the Lessons and Stages of Leadership Development,* Robert Clinton spotlights five phases of leadership development. What he found in his studies of leaders is that many of them stop at phase four. They've built their successful businesses and are looking forward to retirement, when they can kick back and take it easy. That is what they've been working toward their whole life.

But Clinton proposes that every preceding phase in our lives is actually part of our preparation for stage five, which is often after retirement. Every seemingly unrelated event we experience, the people we meet, and the work we do—they're all part of God's preparation to lead us to this next stage. Clinton calls the fifth stage *Convergence.*

Stage five is when we can have the broadest impact. Millennials need us senior leaders of proven moral character to proactively and positively impart wisdom so they get the leadership traction needed to lead well in this rapidly changing culture.

What seemingly unrelated disconnected events have happened over the course of *your* life to date? Really consider that. Perhaps, like me, you've become aware that God is now merging all of your past experiences, talents, skills, and wisdom for a greater purpose.

You are being called to make a difference, and to build our next-gen leaders. More specifically, you have the responsibility to coach and mentor your next-gen leader, the one who comes to mind even as you are reading. This young leader can and will make the difference. You and I play an important role in making that happen. To whom much is given, much is required.

Will you accept the challenge to mentor, coach, and disciple your up-and-coming leader?

I believe that my son's message is a prophetic call, not only for me but for all of us who have the ability to give back. We must not abdicate this responsibility. It's time to shift gears and be intentionally proactive and strategic. Maybe you're thinking, *No one's going to listen to me anyway.*

God inspired the words of the following poem, "The Calling," during a time when I needed strengthening for the journey. In sharing this poem with you, it is my wholehearted prayer that the words will confirm your calling—that you use your uniquely crafted talents to make a difference in the lives of the millennials within your sphere of influence.

The Calling

I am calling you,
I am anointing you,
I am setting you apart for a divine purpose.
Rise up and walk in it.
Turn your back on how you've done it before.
Behold, I am making all things new.
I am opening new vistas and opportunities.
Walk in confidence.

How to Get the Most out of This Book

The ideas I present in the upcoming chapters are designed to help you get, and stay, ahead of the game as you develop and strengthen your next-gen leader. *Millennials Matter* isn't meant to be a prescriptive rule book that you follow to the letter. Instead, it will stimulate your thinking, deepen your understanding of a given topic (especially as it pertains to the cultural arena in which your next-gen leader wants to flourish), and enable you to spark dynamic communication and build a trusting relationship with your mentee.

Here are five tips for how to get the most out of this book:

- **Read Randomly.** Of course, you're welcome to start at page one and read through to the end, but if you prefer, skip around. You'll find practical tips, tools, and talking points to energize and equip you.
- **Share Stories.** I also share stories of experiences provided by my mentors and lessons I've tackled firsthand. These are intended to stimulate your reflection on your own years of leadership development as you exhort, affirm, and encourage your next-gen leader. Share your personal stories with your mentee. Listen to theirs in return. We learn from each other.

- **Ask Questions.** Periodically I'll ask a question to stimulate your reflections. Use those reflections, your own leadership and spiritual experiences, to help build trusting relationships with your next-gen leader.
- **Consider the Spiritual Perspective.** It may help you to more clearly understand my spiritual perspective. I'm an ardent follower of Jesus Christ. I remind myself regularly of the greatest commandment Jesus gave us: "You shall love the Lord your God with all your heart and with all your soul and with all your strength and with all your mind, and [love] your neighbor as yourself" (Luke 10:27 ESV). Love is the ultimate measure of my life, and I believe it's the ultimate measure of each of our lives. Therefore, I strive to ensure that each leadership principle I write about is rooted in Scripture and comes from a serving heart, so that I integrate proven leadership principles with spiritual passion.

  However, like you, I'm on a continual spiritual expedition, and I want to take a learning stance. I don't discount the insights found in other religions and forms of spirituality. I'm a seeker of truth, because all truth is God's truth. On occasion, I quote Scripture from the Bible or refer to personal experiences when I've felt that God was guiding me. This doesn't mean that I disqualify anyone who isn't a Jesus-follower from the potential to be a highly effective character-based leader.
- **Recognize the Individual.** Often, I sit down with millennials and ask, "If there is one thing you feel is most important for experienced leaders to know about you and your generation, what is it?" The first answer I invariably hear is, "I'm not a trend. I'm an individual. Get to know me for who I am."

  As leaders and mentors, we have a unique vantage point to discover what is distinctive about our next-gen leaders and to guide them to develop and leverage those attributes. We are mirrors to them, to opening their eyes to see the strengths of their dreams, motivation, perspectives, and style. During this process we work to draw out the best in each person we work with, and we also tap the best in ourselves. Even though I highlight many trends throughout the book, it's vital to remember that your next-gen leader is an individual, not a trend.

As a final note, *Millennials Matter* was inspired by three important categories of thought:

- **Strengthen Your Character.** Some think character development isn't a problem with millennials. Others hold the opinion that it's insulting to even talk about character development. Yet if we were to ask the ancients, they'd say the development of character and virtue is ongoing, and that character and virtue are at the core of who we are and guide all of our decision making. My belief is that character development is the highest priority for every leader.
- **Lead with Confidence.** Some insist that this generation is confident enough, and we don't have to address this topic with them. I question whether this is true belief in oneself that emanates from the school of hard knocks. Is it confidence based on reality, and able to withstand the shaking of one's core values? All leaders grapple with their self-assuredness when it is rattled and tested. Those whose confidence stems from a solid foundation will become stronger in the crucible and become even more confident over time.
- **Engage in Collaboration.** Many argue that millennials are experts at collaboration, that they've been instructed in the importance of teamwork. It's easy to collaborate

with people who have similar values, but what happens when team members have diverse values and ways of thinking? Do millennials seek to understand, or do they quickly discount other perspectives? Remember the story of the elephant? One person says the elephant is shaped like a snake, and the other says it is shaped like a wall. Only when they bring their perspectives together can they agree. True collaboration happens when we respect and seek to understand every team-mate's viewpoint.

With that in mind, it's time to shift gears.

1

Why Millennials Matter

Millennials. They're one of the most talked-about, written-about, and agonized-about generations of all time. Born between 1980 and the mid-2000s, they'll comprise more than 50 percent of the workforce by 2020.[1] To ensure vibrant, thriving business growth, we need to tap their strengths.

The 2017 Bloomberg article, "A Quarter of Millennials Who Live at Home Don't Work—or Study," reveals just how many young people have difficulty placing themselves on a career path:

- Approximately 33 percent of eighteen- to thirty-four-year-olds live at home or in college dormitories.
- Of those twenty-five- to thirty-four-year-olds who live with their parents, 25 percent neither work nor are enrolled in school—that's 2.2 million millennials in the United States.[2]

In the 2016 Inc.com article "29 Surprising Facts That Explain Why Millennials See the World Differently," author Gordon Tredgold presented statistics to help us understand what drives this generation:

- 35 percent of employed millennials have started their own businesses on the side to supplement their incomes.
- 54 percent either want to start a business or already have.
- 64 percent of millennials would rather make $40,000 a year at a job they love than $100,000 a year at a job they think is boring.

- 69 percent believe regular office attendance is unnecessary.
- 74 percent want flexible work schedules.
- 80 percent say they prefer on-the-spot recognition over formal reviews and feel this recognition is imperative for their growth and understanding of their job.
- 84 percent say that helping to make a positive difference in the world is more important than professional recognition.
- 88 percent prefer a collaborative work culture rather than a competitive one.
- 92 percent believe that business success should be measured by more than just profit.[3]

When I ask experienced business leaders how they see the millennial generation, I either hear glowing praise or intense frustration, rarely anything in between. This is a fascinating trend with this generation.

Dennis Thum, chaplain at the University of Sioux Falls, gave me this analogy:

I think of it as a camel. When you interact with the first hump, you see impressive, emerging leaders that give you great hope for the future of the world. Then when you talk with those from the second hump, you see people who appear to be lost, without hope.

Some are coming from the stereotypical background of entitlement and overprotection (helicopter parents). Some are simply distracted by the hedonistic and materialistic milieu in which they have been raised and are not ready to grow up. Some are badly wounded by life's complexities, such as children of divorce, the Great Recession, and parental addiction issues. It appears that many aren't sure that there is hope. When you have been raised in a very difficult situation and haven't had anyone to serve as a mentor or guide, it's difficult to know who you can trust.

In a recent survey, our company, Sales Growth Specialists, asked business leaders to list all the frustrations they experience in working with millennials. Business owners, CEOs, presidents, and business advisors responded—271 of them. Of those, 60 percent said they have deep concerns with how to work with this generation.

The top three response categories were:

- Character traits (45 percent)
- Confidence (34 percent)
- Collaboration (21 percent)

Their strongest complaints were the following:

- Lack of determination and resiliency (22 percent)
- Lack of accountability (17 percent)
- A know-it-all attitude (14 percent)
- Disregard for the value of work (12 percent)
- Low conflict-resolution skills (9 percent)

Many millennials tend to be overeducated, underemployed, and heavily in debt. Their childhoods were generally filled with praise, but lacking the investment of positive role models. With extensive knowledge available at their fingertips, most appear to have plenty of confidence. But it's artificial maturity, not earned confidence based on practical everyday experience.[4] In a world of increasing diversity, some millennials shut down communication, instead of collaborating, when dealing with conflict and differences.

A WORD FROM A MILLENNIAL …

"I want to talk to you about this word *millennial*. It's so loaded. It carries a dismissive and negative connotation and causes me to check out. What if we just referred to them as the 'next wave of youth' or something that conjures more hope for our future?"

Most of the young people I know and coach are impressive, emerging leaders from the first hump of the camel. In fact, they experience hurt, even victimization, when generalizations about their age group ignore the promising leadership potential that many possess. They're intentional in forming solid character that can weather rapid change. They're eager to build authentic confidence. And they know the importance of really listening and valuing others so that synergistic collaboration happens. These young people, even ones who are struggling to find their place, give me great hope for future generations.

The millennials you coach in your place of business will all be unique, as are you. Turn a sharp eye to what is distinctive in every mentee. By observing their individual strengths, you'll draw out the best in each of them. You know from experience that a truly successful team, one that can survive global and financial turmoil, requires an amalgamation of singular abilities.

Let's start discovering theirs.

Millennials: A Present-Day Plan to Maximize Your Business

I'm a sales-growth expert and business consultant. One of our most important sales-growth strategies is hiring and retaining sales pros who have "hunting" DNA. We teach companies how to source and develop these star performers so they consistently prospect and win new accounts.

The star performers responsible for the growth of your business, will, in a few short years, be primarily millennials. That's a significant reason why mentoring young people needs to be a top priority of every company's business growth strategy.

We need to actively recruit them to replace the retiring baby boomers.

Starting in the early 2020s, millennials are going to drive our economy, and they will continue to do so for thirty years. Since that is the case, millennials will be a key asset to continual business growth. So how do we tap the millennial potential?

First, millennials are digital natives. They have a unique perspective on how to leverage technology and the social selling world for a new, competitive edge. Some experienced leaders have told me they feel a bit intimidated by all the technical knowledge and savvy of the younger generation.

First, don't feel intimidated! Ask them for advice on solving your technical problems. Listen to their ideas about new communication strategies. With unlimited knowledge at their fingertips, they can quickly find an answer to anything.

Second, along with their digital connectivity, millennials grew up in a global world. They are often independent thinkers open to asking tough questions. They're not afraid to confront long-standing paradigms.

To remain successful in a hyper-competitive marketplace, we need to constantly rethink our strategies. Yesterday's proven practices no long deliver the same results. The millennial prospective could provide the competitive advantage your business needs as you seek to grow your market share.

But Danita, you might be thinking, *millennials lack real-life experience.*

Yes, millennials are more comfortable with technology than our generation is, but they may not know how to leverage it to grow sales, take market share, or scale a business.

That's where leadership is vital; they urgently need our generation's top-tier leaders to invest in them. We learned the hard way the importance of having strong internal character with deeply rooted confidence, honoring our work as integral to our life's calling, and collaborating with others to achieve sought-after dreams. We know we must be clear on our values so that we can make solid decisions, both personally and professionally.

Millennials are poised to become assets to our businesses. Our investment of time and wisdom will help the next generation develop their full potential.

Millennials: A Forward-Looking Plan to Mobilize Your Leaders

Researchers project that nearly 80 percent of current business leaders and CEOs will retire within the next ten years.[5] But the fact is, 100 percent of current leaders and senior management will retire eventually. Each one will take with them decades of experience and wisdom.

Irrespective of the size of your business, take the time to create a transition plan to ensure your company will continue to reap the rewards of the blood and sweat you've invested over the years. That's good stewardship. This plan needs to include the identification and mentoring of suitable millennials to replace your experienced workforce.

It's a win-win strategy, in which you and your next-gen leader both win. You win by maximizing your business, mobilizing your trailblazers, and realizing your leadership legacy. Your next-gen leader wins in that they learn from a seasoned leader respected as wise. It's a powerful combination when young talent and wise leadership come together to work toward a shared vision and mutual goals.

Look at this situation from a buyer's perspective. If they see your successful business run by aging baby boomers in all key management positions, with no millennials in various stages of readiness, it could affect the buyer's decision to invest or buy. You might be sacrificing your entire life's work and financial nest egg because you can't let go.

Be sure to start the business transition process early so you don't find yourself in a predicament one day. Ramp up your efforts to mentor millennials for leadership roles in your business.

Two-Way Mentoring: Learn from the Learner While You Teach

Many people think coaching and mentoring are more or less the same thing. They're not. Take a look at the following differentiators and how they might impact your strategies for development of the millennials on your team.

Coaching is usually a short-term exercise. It focuses on concrete issues such as acquiring effective talking and listening skills, strategic thinking, and effective management. A capable, immediate manager is the ideal person to coach the young team member.

Mentoring is an ongoing, long-term trust-building strategy. It's more about creating a safe environment where issues (even sensitive ones) can be openly shared and discussed and solutions can be found. This may include personal and professional challenges in self-image, self-confidence, and the work-life balance. The mentor can be someone outside the mentee's direct working environment.

Neither coaching nor mentoring millennials is for the fainthearted. They require courage and feel arduous, demanding, and even burdensome at times.

My best advice is to be willing to learn from each experience. During a discussion with one of my daughters, I realized that I was running the risk of becoming too set in my views about a number of subjects (we were discussing politics at the time). Our conversation highlighted the importance for all leaders to be willing to see things they feel strongly about from a different perspective.

Even if I don't change my point of view, I still need to keep an open mind and be willing to, at the very least, broaden my frame of reference.

A WORD FROM A MILLENNIAL …

"Millennials don't want to feel like projects for the previous generation to fix, in part because we often feel like the previous generation is the one that needs fixing. Mentoring the next-gen leader has to be a two-way street. The conversations have to give and take, and to cultivate respect, the leader must extend respect."

Here's some great news. Based on my personal experience in mentoring young leaders, millennials welcome mentoring and coaching from people they respect.

Millennials want to be with honest, authentic leaders; favor a trusting, transparent relationship with their superiors; and work best with clear guidelines and frequent feedback.

Millennials also love being able to teach their mentor something. When you bring them into brainstorming and problem-solving processes, millennials shine. I've strengthened trust in many relationships I'm building with up-and-coming leaders by asking for their perspectives on a range of topics. One of my favorite questions to ask is about the latest apps they've found that will make my life easier. Besides knowing about the trendy time-saving apps, they have important insights for us to consider that test and rethink our own paradigms on a range of topics, from local to global.

Even in the writing of this book, I reached out to several millennials I trust and respect to get their feedback and perceptions. They are my Millennial Reviewer Team. Their perspectives were invaluable, and I'm deeply indebted to them for sharing their views.

Quick story. I called my first millennial leadership coaching group "The Joshua Initiative." Where did that name come from? In the ancient world, a great patriarch, Moses, mentored another great leader, Joshua. As we look at today's challenges locally, regionally, nationally, and globally, we know that we need strong, wise leaders like Joshua. However, Joshua became a Joshua because he had a Moses, someone who invested years of his life pouring into Joshua. Vice versa, Moses became a Moses because there was a Joshua. We cannot expect the Joshuas of this generation to lead the charge into the future without there being a Moses. Will you be that Moses for the Joshuas waiting for you in your life?

This two-way mentoring strategy will be as much of a growth experience for you as it will be for your young mentee. An instructor who cannot learn should not teach.

LEADERSHIP LESSON

Open your eyes, ears, and heart to see who are the up-and-coming leaders in your sphere of influence who might be open to a relationship with you.

Section 1

Strengthen Character

Courage is contagious.
When a brave man takes a stand,
the spines of others are
often stiffened.

—Billy Graham

Part 1

Cultivate a Courageous Core

Definition: A center of character strength that provides a firm footing so that one has a positive influence.

Determination
Awareness
Knowledge
Optimism
Trustworthiness
Accountability

2

A Courageous Character Core and Leadership

A courageous core is the center of character strength. It provides stable footing so you can impart a positive influence. Throughout my growing-up years, several key people of strong character invested in my personal and leadership development. I am humbly indebted to my parents, my youth group leader at church, my piano teacher, my first boss at Dairy Queen, the president at the University of Sioux Falls, and my first manager at Xerox Corporation.

An important lesson I learned from this diverse group of mentors is that inward integrity is much more important than outward image. Their impact and influence keeps expanding, even today. That is the reward of wise, sustainable leadership.

A WORD FROM A MILLENNIAL ...

"Millennials care a lot about character development. Finding balance, addressing the whole person, seeking holistic growth, and not segregating our personal and professional lives are things that are important to millennials. For me and many of my friends, we talk about wanting to learn from other, more experienced leaders. We want to learn and grow; however, I don't think we arrive at this the same way as those in previous generations did. We know there's always more we don't know and more we could do with new information. So I think millennials are willing and motivated to come to the table and explore character development."

The Character and Courage Leadership Framework

On our recent "Millennial Matters" survey, 45 percent of business leaders, CEOs, presidents, and business advisors indicated that issues of character were a concern with their up-and-coming leaders. So this is an important place to start. We know that everything we are and do emanates from our core character.

Developing our character core is as important as developing our physical core. A strong physical core leads to better balance and stability; we have the power to do the activities we want to do when we want to do them. In fact, a strong physical core underpins everything we do.

When leaders are healthy on the inside and operate with both high character and high courage, they have a positive influence and are constructive change agents. This group of leaders has a willingness to take responsible risks and communicate authentically with their teams. This balance of character and courage is foundational to their confidence.

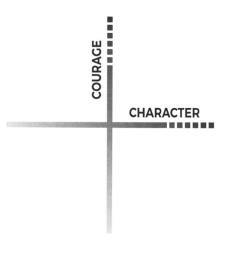

Unfortunately, not all leaders operate with both character and courage. We sometimes meet and work with people who are lacking one or the other. These leaders don't last long. They have little influence, avoid daunting difficulties, and fail to gain the respect of those they lead.

One of these groups of leaders might be courageous, bravely tackling the mountains of obstacles in front of them, but due to weak character, their motives are compromised. No one trusts them. They may have a disregard for people, either internal colleagues or external clients. They may deliver short-term results, but the trail of destroyed relationships and the negative impact on their company brands can be disastrous.

Conversely, a group of leaders with strong character foundations can be trusted to do the morally correct thing at all times. However, due to a lack of courage, these leaders have little, if any, influence on decisions. Their voices are limited because they're afraid to exercise boldness.

Your next-gen leader's character core will influence how they will handle relationships, tackle new responsibilities, and approach leadership roles. In the end, character determines the leader's ability to achieve lasting results that stand the test of time.

Why Is Cultivating a Character Core Important for Your Next-Gen Leader?

When I raise the issue of cultivating character in our young leaders, I get a variety of reactions:

- "Isn't character a given? It seems a waste of time to talk about it."
- "Isn't it insulting to talk to young leaders about character development? They're out of grade school and high school, so we don't need to have a Character Counts! program."

- "I don't see character as a problem. Now there are other problems—such as their feeling of entitlement, lack of appreciation for what others do for them, and having their short-term needs outweigh long-term thinking—but not character."

When I posed these responses to Phyllis Hennecy Hendry, president and CEO of Lead Like Jesus, who works extensively with millennials, her reply was quick: "Just look historically at some of the things that have happened in business, here and around the world. The failures that have happened in business most often do not come from doing something wrong in the business. It comes from a character failure or a flaw from the leader."

She went on to say, "I heard a quote recently from a church staff, but it applies to any organization. 'Who our church becomes tomorrow, is who our staff becomes today.' Any business would have to say that also. So if we're not developing a staff with character, we are looking at a future that is going to be devastated by those who have not kept the kind of character that we would have hoped for our organization."

In the olden days, character development started early in life. I'm in awe of the character and grit of the hard-working people who first settled in my home state, North Dakota. The internal strength of character, the backbone that inspired them to weather the ferociousness of the Northern Plains, runs deep in our local culture.

Having grown up on The Triple T Ranch in North Dakota, I resonate with the Code of the West, the following ten principles listed by the Center for Cowboy Ethics and Leadership. Although this code was enacted more than a century ago, the principles apply to all of us. Why? Because they were founded on the ancient virtues.

1. Live each day with courage.
2. Take pride in your work.

3. Always finish what you start.
4. Do what has to be done.
5. Be tough, but fair.
6. When you make a promise, keep it.
7. Ride for the brand.
8. Talk less and say more.
9. Remember that some things aren't for sale.
10. Know where to draw the line.[1]

This internal sense of right and wrong was instilled in many of us across America, regardless of our heritage and roots. We knew that character strength came from within.

However, much of leadership theory and practice over the past couple of decades has focused on external appearances or the "right" personality traits. Other leadership streams focus on how we accomplish our leadership responsibilities, admonishing leaders to develop with the right leadership competencies, skill sets, or emotional IQ. The topic of the leader's deep moral fiber and character is rarely discussed. It's almost as if it's a non-issue.

And yet Doug Lennick and Fred Kiel, PhD, after doing extensive research, concluded, "Strong moral skills are not only an essential element of successful leadership, but are also a business advantage. The most trustworthy leaders in any company are likely to be trustworthy individuals who have a strong set of moral beliefs and the ability to put them into action. Furthermore, even in a world that occasionally rewards bad behavior, the fastest way to build a successful business is to hire those people who have the highest moral and ethical skills you can find."[2]

This question of why it is important to build a strong character core in your next-gen leader brings me to the rarely recognized ancient wisdom found in the cardinal virtues of practical, everyday living. These virtues—prudence, justice, temperance, and courage—were derived primarily from Aristotle.

Along with these, the church has long held the view that there are three core theological virtues—faith, hope, and charity—that have stood the test of time.

Virtue seems like an outdated word, but it's time to revive it. We need to integrate virtues into our companies. Many shy away from this because virtues are hard to ask about and equally hard to measure. Recognizing the foundational value of virtues in wise leadership, some universities are becoming more intentional. The University of Mary in Bismarck, North Dakota, recently launched a new MBA (Master of Business Administration) track called Virtuous Leadership. The University of Sioux Falls builds virtues into their student wellness initiatives. Bethel University in St. Paul, Minnesota, integrates the study of virtues in their Transformational Leadership degree program.

Here is how N. T. Wright, Anglican Bishop of Durham, describes virtue: "Virtue is … to do something which is good and right, but which doesn't come naturally. And then, on the thousand and first time, when it really matters, they find that they do what's required automatically. Virtue is what happens when wise and courageous choices become second nature."[3]

So how do we translate these ancient virtues and wisdoms into modern-day non-cowboy vernacular so that both we and our mentees "get it"? How might you work with your next-gen leader to grasp these difficult ideas so they execute naturally on the thousandth time?

DAKOTA is a tool I use to facilitate and describe this translation process. It's based upon my appreciation for my North Dakota roots, and I hope it's a useful guide as you work with your millennial leader to help them develop a strong, courageous core:

- Determination
- Awareness
- Knowing

- Optimism
- Trustworthiness
- Accountability

A WORD FROM A MILLENNIAL ...

"Many millennials have serious objections to learning character development from the previous generation. Leaders will have to grapple with this as they work to influence and mentor the new generation, because they may find they don't have as much credibility with their audience as they want or think they deserve. For example, corporate social responsibility. My internal cynic says, 'Why would I listen to you talk about responsibility and the right thing to do when your generation signed off on decisions and business practices I don't agree with?' I think it's important for leaders to understand they have their work cut out for them in establishing credibility and gaining respect from the millennials they are trying to mentor and lead."

LEADERSHIP LESSON

Nurture a courageous character core in your mentee.
It provides a firm foundation for being
a positive change agent.

Determination: One Step Closer to Character

There was nothing glamorous about it. I grew up on a cattle ranch. Not a sprawling, luxurious ranch a movie star buys to escape his crazy life. This was more like the conditions Laura Ingalls Wilder wrote about in *Little House on the Prairie.* It was an eight-hundred-square-foot tar-papered homestead shack with no running water. I used an outhouse every day until I was thirteen years old.

My dad, or "Super Dad" as I call him, worked three jobs to provide for the family and to fuel my parents' dream of owning a cattle ranch. My mom, aka "Super Mom," had four children under the age of five. She washed laundry with a wringer washing machine, froze vegetables from the garden, picked berries and made jelly, raised geese, and more. It was a tough, exhausting life.

Part of the reason Mom gardened was for survival if the electricity went out—or, should I say, *when*. A strong winter blizzard could leave us without power and isolated for weeks. And that's exactly what happened in March 1966. We endured one of the most severe blizzards ever recorded. One snow bank outside our house stood ten feet high. We were snowed in for a week and a half. Throughout the Northern Plains, approximately 74,500 head of cattle, 54,000 sheep, and 2,400 hogs died in that storm.

North Dakota conditions were tough, but my parents had

unshakable determination that they could make it. They were committed to pursue their vision and goals despite physical hardships, financial setbacks, and multiple roadblocks. They personified determination.

Many gave up and left those taxing conditions, but my parents stayed on the land, working hard every day to pursue their goals. Trusting in God, they made The Triple T Ranch a dream come true, and it is thriving to this day. It offers guests a warm, hospitable home away from home to relax, rejuvenate, and enjoy nature. During hunting season, the vast land offers some of the best pheasant, sharp tail, and whitetail hunting in all of western North Dakota.

Who are some of the role models who have inspired you to develop determination as part of your character strength? How did you learn this virtue?

A WORD FROM A MILLENNIAL ...

"I think you can define determination as stubbornly trudging forward to achieve a goal, maintaining an understanding of possible rewards as motivation, sticking to your values no matter what, and rolling with the punches."

Millennials and Determination

Seasoned leaders who I coach often ask a legitimate question: "Does the next-gen leader I'm working with have what it takes to be successful in their current role and to build a career? Will they be able to carry forward and implement the strategies we have in place?"

Life is more comfortable for most of us these days, with luxuries such as having indoor plumbing. Even so, I'm keenly aware of the difficult hardships young leaders face today as they navigate both successes and setbacks. In my coaching and mentoring of millennials, I find they deal with life in different ways.

Some millennials exhibit a lack of resiliency. At its root, this is a lack of the character trait of determination. That's one of the concerns continually raised in *The Chronicle of Higher Education*,[1] which is regarded as the best source of news, information, and jobs for college and university faculty members and administrators. There's a growing trend of students, especially those on the second hump of the camel, who are afraid to take risks and need to be certain about something before moving forward. Failure can be seen as catastrophic and unacceptable; helicopter parenting is often the culprit. However, the experts admit that this parenting phenomenon is due, in part, to our "helicopter society."[2] We are being fed a constant barrage of stories that shake the confidence of most any reasonable parent.

Some say the problem is that millennials have been raised by "peer-ents"[3] (parents who are more like peers than they are parents). This is in contrast to a healthier parenting structure where there is strong accountability and high standards, coupled with a strong support system and copious encouragement.

Determination is the character quality needed to fuel resoluteness as millennials face modern-day realities. Regardless of what their family dynamics were, or are, they are now in the workforce. Determination and mental toughness are prized qualities that often get noticed and rewarded quickly.

A WORD FROM A MILLENNIAL …

"Determination for me is very connected to the *why*. Money and success in a corporate career are not enough of a *why* for a lot of young people I know. So, they (and I) bounce around a bit."

Regardless of where millennials are on the determination spectrum, how might we help them develop this strength even further?

How to Build Determination in Your Next-Gen Leader

Share Stories

Think about times when you tackled an extremely difficult task. What kept you moving forward even though the task was incredibly demanding?

- Reflect on the principles, skills, and mind-sets you've developed over the years.
- Consider how these experiences might inspire your next-gen leader's capacity to deal with the obstacles they are facing.
- Tell them your story, authentically. Be willing to talk about your fears and failures. For your next-gen leader, authenticity counts. They want to know what motivated you to push through the discouragement. Was the failure a waste of time for you? Or, did you find it to be a rich gift of direction?
- Ask your mentee how your experiences might apply to their current situation. Then listen and ask questions to understand their perspectives.
- Listen to their stories of determination, when they have struggled to meet their goals and objectives. Applaud their journey.

A WORD FROM A MILLENNIAL ...

"This tip is *so good*! I'm never as inspired as when I'm hearing from a leader how they persevered *while petrified*. We need to know that failure doesn't have to debilitate."

Clarify Values

I use a values tournament to help young leaders get a better grasp on what really matters to them. We start the tournament with sixty words. Through discussions and discovery, the lists are shortened to the top five values for that specific person. Gaining clarity on what's important to them helps with the following:

- Values guide decisions. Millennials are more apt to base decisions on their own internal compasses and not on peer pressure or other external pressures.
- Values increase confidence. When millennials are clear about their values, especially when they write them down, it's easier to find the courage and confidence to make and stick to wiser choices.
- Values improve emotional stamina. When people are knocked down, whether it's being criticized at work, fired from jobs, or ostracized by friends, values can be a plumb line, helping them decipher whether or not they're on the right path. If yes, get up and keep moving forward. If not, commit to making needed changes. Then get up and get moving.

Work Out the Determination Muscle

Strengthening the determination muscle takes time. How do we build that muscle? It may start with just one small activity that your mentee commits to doing for the next thirty days, such as the following:

- Go to the gym every day or set aside time for meditation.
- Commit to a certain amount of outbound phone calls for the week, regardless of the obstacles.
- Practice a new listening technique and keep track of successes and failures.

All of these examples include an activity that stretches mentees' current comfort zones. Thus, they include victories to celebrate. When your young leader gets knocked down or stumbles, you're there to help pick them up so they get back on track. As you help them, ask for their help in supporting you where you're stretching your own comfort zone and strengthening your own determination muscles.

Determination is one my favorite qualities. Personally, I think it's one of my favorite concepts, because it reminds me of all the crazy times growing up with no running water. That means I had to use the outhouse whether it was 110 degrees above or 10 degrees below zero. I had to use it whether there were driving rains, sleet, or blizzard conditions. It nurtured grit and mental toughness. These are the qualities you can help build into your next-gen leader.

LEADERSHIP LESSON

Determination fuels a courageous character
that can weather uncertainty, challenges, and chaos.

4

Awareness:
The Key to Activate
Understanding

Early one morning I stood in front of my closet, contemplating my lineup of corporate navy blue suits. With various fabrics and styles, each served its own purpose—the First Call Suit, the Presentation Suit, the Closing Suit. Suddenly, it hit me. I'd been donning these beautifully tailored suits as if they were my armor, protecting me from the harshness of the real workday world.

Ironically, these suits also masked the real Danita, from myself as well as from prospects and customers. On the outside, the got-my-act-together armor looked nice and shiny, like I fit in the corporate world. On the inside, the situation was darker and more chaotic. I wrestled with how to be Super Sales Leader, Super Parent, and Super Spouse all at the same time. Like a broken record, I asked myself over and over, "How can I do it? How can I excel at a high-pressure corporate career and be the best wife to Gordon and best mom to three young school children? Others do it. Come on, Danita, you can figure this out!" Of course, like every mom, I felt guilty about not being a good-enough spouse, parent, friend, daughter, soccer coach, classroom helper ... and the list went on.

Standing in front of the mirror in my navy blue armor, I realized I was exhausted. I'd been pulled in too many directions for too long, all while hiding and giving in to the expectations of others. I made a personal vow to learn more about who I was and what I was called to do. In a symbolic gesture, I also did something radical. I burned one of my suits. By doing so, I committed to start the freeing transition to live life as the real Danita. It was a powerful awareness moment for me.

When did this moment happen for you? When did you realize you couldn't live someone else's life, that you needed to live your own? Who supported you through this journey? Ironically, it's only when we have this crucial awareness that the authentic, powerful leader within us can emerge.

What exactly is awareness, as used in the context of leadership? Awareness is the capacity to gain knowledge about the unique components of our character, and is reflected in how we apply that information in our leadership, personal, and spiritual interactions. The virtues required to sustain a healthy awareness capability include faith, temperance, prudence, and love.

Millennials and Awareness

The millennial generation experiences some of the same hurdles we dealt with growing up. Plus, they have the added difficulty of living in a media-saturated world. Every day they're buried in an avalanche of commercials, print ads, brand labels, social media posts, Google ads, and notifications on their phones. Often, marketers believe using any method to get their attention and entice them to purchase is fair play; companies are increasingly using artificial intelligence with advanced algorithms to strategically hyper-target each individual person. Digital marketing experts estimate we're each exposed to three thousand to twenty thousand messages per day.[1]

Each message touts *their* product or service as the only way to live life to the fullest, whether it's brushing with the right toothpaste, wearing the right clothes, or buying the right phone. Every day, millennials are bombarded with subtle and not-so-subtle marketing messages of who they should be, what they should look like, and what they should care about.

The noise of it all is deafening and brutally distracting. And more than ever before, ads are deceitful. All these conflicting messages sidetrack next-gen leaders from developing keen awareness of who they really are and what they are uniquely called to do.

A WORD FROM A MILLENNIAL …

"I think it might be hard for millennials to know who they are because many of us grew up being told we could be whoever we want to be. We don't know how to separate what is uniquely sacred in ourselves from what can be changed. Assessments and surveys can give us a language to talk about our tendencies, but I've found it helpful to focus on the type of person I want to be. Then to live toward that."

I enjoyed a recent conversation with a clinical psychologist who works with business owners and leaders. He shared this insight: "All the stuff the baby boomers have sought—big house, big cars, big toys, big vacations—is not about greed. It's about identity. People are desperately trying to get affirmation that they are okay." The process of becoming more fully aware of who we are, what our identity is, and what we are called to do, is the awareness journey each of us must take.

How to Activate Awareness
in Your Next-Gen Leader

Around the time of my navy blue suit experience, I wrote these words on the back of a business card: *I am exactly who I am supposed to be. I am a woman made in God's image. I have been strategically called to particular people, places, and situations to accomplish God's purposes and plans.* I regularly reread those words to keep me focused and grounded.

A WORD FROM A MILLENNIAL ...

"Interesting. Many millennials grew up in the raise-their-self-esteem movement that started in the '80s. For me, it's not about how special I am but about the humility of recognizing that it's about God's purposes and plans, not my potentially self-centered goals."

I believe that many millennials would be inspired by the mantra on my tattered business card. As the up-and-coming leader you are coaching begins to get clarity on their purpose, invite them to create their own personal mantra. Have them write it down, review it, post it somewhere they will see it often, and make it a new part of their daily focus. Millennials aren't often invited to critically think differently about what they are thinking. You should also share key times in your life where you have had to change your thinking in order to be more productive. Here are three more ways to activate awareness in your next-gen leader.

Focus Inward

Persuade your mentee to take a personality test like Strengths-Finder or DiSC. If you haven't taken one recently, do it yourself too. Share your results with them, both your strengths as well as your potential weaknesses. Ask for their reflections on their results. Explore what resonated with them, what surprised them, and what made them feel cautious or weak. This will help them gain more awareness of their natural gifts and talents.

Focus Outward

After your mentee receives their personality results, discuss how the strengths they identified can be leveraged in the following areas:

- Sales conversations
- Client relationships
- Team collaboration
- Leadership responsibilities

Suggest they talk about their experiences with you or another mentor who will motivate them to lean into these strengths to accomplish their personal and business goals. Tell them how you learned to leverage your gifts. Remember to include both your victories and defeats when telling your story.

Focus Upward

Invite your next-gen leader to reflect on how their strengths and weaknesses impact their spiritual life. This level of awareness will help them recognize and treasure those transcendent moments.

A WORD FROM A MILLENNIAL ...

Corporate social responsibility and a millennial's desire to work with companies pursuing social good is evident all around. We desire to grow as a whole person, and we don't divorce spiritual and social connections from our professional lives."

Help your young leader become aware of their "navy blue suits." What are they holding onto as an unnecessary part of their identity? Through the resulting epiphanies, they can develop boldness and strength from within.

LEADERSHIP LESSON

Character is strengthened as you
bolster awareness of yourself,
those in your community, and God.

5

Knowledge: Deep Knowing Boosts Moral Fiber

"It's really a war of good against evil."

I was in a packed house for the Leadership ND (North Dakota) Cyber Security Summit with key business, education, health, and government leaders. The keynote speaker's words caused me to shift uneasily in my chair as I considered the risks of a cyberattack on our businesses. It could affect our integrity as well as national security. When the speaker said, "It's really a war of good against evil," a chill crawled up my spine.

As leaders, we concurred that for the health and vitality of our families, businesses, state, and nation, we needed to take the necessary steps to protect ourselves from a cyberattack. Even more important, we needed to invest in raising future leaders with strong moral fiber.

We need leaders who know what is right and what is wrong— leaders who have the courage to stand for what is right over what is easy.

A WORD FROM A MILLENNIAL ...

"We see ourselves as global citizens, as small pieces in a single much-larger puzzle. We aren't okay with shrinking our perspectives to fit inside white picket fences when there are injustices being committed to our brothers and sisters around the world. We have a great sense of responsibility to stand up for those who are targeted and disregarded by the majority, regardless of what language they speak or where they come from."

Millennials and Knowing What Is Right

What are you seeing in the moral fiber of your next-gen leader? Do you see the courage to stand up for what is right over what is easy? Before answering, consider some of the following major events that happened during the formative years of this generation:

- Corporate corruption scandals, such as Enron and WorldCom
- Tragic events, like the massacre at Columbine High School in Colorado
- Rising education costs with high student loan debt
- Terrorist attacks around the globe

How did events like these impact the generation of emerging leaders? Many say millennials are more aware of the value of family and the brevity of life. On 9/11, our youngest millennials were in preschool and our oldest ones were twenty-one years old. That means the majority of millennials will forever remember this tragic moment in our nation's history. This, plus other global tragedies broadcast on news stations 24/7, left a mark on young minds during critical formative years when they learned to define what is right and what is wrong.

Many parents of millennials reacted to the events of the world with fear. They doubled down and dug into their careers in order to ensure their children a better future. Some of us, due to the pressure and stress, inadvertently delegated character development and the strengthening of moral fiber to others.

Deep knowing boosts moral fiber. Lack of knowing can prevent it.

A WORD FROM A MILLENNIAL ...

"Millennials often see leaders from the previous generation as the single bottom-line thinkers that justified false
advertising, pollution, factory farming, and human rights
violations. We see them as having lost much of their
credibility when it comes to talking about the right thing
to do."

Tedi Anne Hasapopoulos, business ethics professor at Bethel
University in St. Paul, Minnesota, instructs millennials in ethics.
Her perspective is insightful in helping us think through how
to activate our next-gen leaders in developing the deep knowing
that boosts moral fiber. When asked to describe the task before
us, here is what Professor Hasapopoulos had to say:

As I think about the ways in which I teach ethics to millennials, I talk to them about the values foundation on
which they set their moral footings. How wide, deep,
and long is it? What kind of material is it comprised of?
Is it the size and thickness of a postage stamp or wide and
deep as a foundation block? Is it solid granite or shifting
sand? Our values are the basis on which we make moral
decisions. Unless our values are grounded in something
solid, we will stumble when pushed by ethical adversity.
That's why so many people experience moral failure. It is
not because they're awful people. It is because they were
too easily pushed over.

So how does a person build a wide, long, and deep
foundation of knowing what is right, so they can stand
upon that knowing when ethical decisions are to be
made? Aristotle said we must habitually practice the
cardinal virtues of prudence, justice, temperance, and
courage. If we practice these consistently in everyday life,

then they become the go-to position when ethical pressure exerts its negative force. So don't wait until you need virtue to develop virtue. It'll be too late by then.

How does one develop virtue? That is where the three Christian virtues enter the picture—deeper faith, greater hope, and more expansive love. For Christians, all these virtues are developed in three major ways. First, we allow God's Word, the Bible, to instruct us as to what is virtuous. Second, we allow the exemplar of Jesus, who we can read about in the Bible, to demonstrate virtue in action. Third, we open ourselves to the directing of the Holy Spirit to develop the "fruit" of love, joy, patience, kindness, gentleness, faithfulness, moral goodness, and self-control (Galatians 5:22–23). We can do this through focus, effort, and prayer that God will help us develop them. This spurs knowledge and sharpens it.

Virtue is solidified by practice. We practice what the Bible instructs and what Jesus did, and do what the Holy Spirit directs us toward, even in the little things that seem to have minimal moral consequences. Through those steps we build up our moral muscle in preparation for standing against moral decisions that can bring significant harm.

How to Boost Moral Fiber
in Your Next-Gen Leader

Morals are personal and internal, whereas ethics are societal and external. Professor Hasapopoulos's moral foundation-footings imagery is helpful for us as we talk about ethics, which is often a sensitive topic where we can get branded as old school or out of touch with today's culture. I recommend developing a list of questions that your next-gen leader can ask when they get into a compromising situation. Here are some ideas to add to your own to help them jumpstart their personal list.

- **What are the facts?** Discernment in a difficult situation requires examination of all the relevant facts. Fear or other intense emotions cloud the facts. Invite your mentee to put on their investigator's hat and do the following:
  - gather information by asking who, what, where, when, why, and how questions;
  - talk to all the stakeholders to get a broader and deeper understanding of the situation; and
  - listen for emotion in others, which may cloud their perception of the facts as they remember.
- **What is the ethical dilemma?** Sometimes what we call an ethical dilemma is really just a personal choice or preference that is different from our own. In a culture of moral relativism, it can be difficult to determine what actions are within the scope of personal preferences and which are in conflict with ancient virtues. Guide your future leader through ethical dilemmas until you are confident in their standing. This can be hard work, but it is important work for a young leader to do.
- **What are the alternatives?** Sometimes people get stuck thinking that the only way to solve a problem is to do it by compromising their ethics. However, when we start brainstorming options on how to solve the problem, we'll often develop a whole cadre of options along the ethical scale. Many of these will be more aligned with our values and character. Others will be ruled out because they don't support virtuous leadership. Work with your mentee to recognize and act on ethics-based alternatives to problem solving.
- **What are the possible consequences?** When wrestling with options, it's a good test to consider the results—what would happen after a particular action. Recognizing the intended and unintended consequences of a dilemma can help inform a wiser course of

action. Urge your leader to consider results and unintended consequences prior to making decisions.

What are some questions that you would invite your mentee to consider adding to their ethical guideline list?

- **Are you acting responsibly?** *Responsible* is defined as being able to act without supervision. Knowing what is right and doing what is right aren't always easy. There are a multitude of mini decisions that inform any decision. Theological ethicist H. Richard Niebuhr taught that responsible people have three qualities: they initiate action, respond to situations, and are accountable. Teach your up-and-coming leader to model these qualities to ensure they will continually gain ground through their responsibility.

Knowledge, a deep knowing that boosts moral character, requires exceptional courage and internal capacity that values others to such a degree that we will always do what is right over what is easy. This character trait requires all seven virtues.

Ancient patriarchs before Aristotle—Moses, Joshua, and King David—talked of the war that's raging for what is morally and ethically superior. That war continues to rage in every human being, in every culture, and in every leader.

LEADERSHIP LESSON

Invest in building a future leader with
strong moral fiber who has the courage
to stand for what is right over what is easy.

6

Optimism:
An Activating Force

"Dad, what was the worst stuck tractor you ever had to deal with?" I asked during an after-dinner conversation while at The Triple T Ranch.

He immediately knew. No hesitation.

It was December of 1979, and he'd just invested in a brand-new John Deere tractor. It was beautiful, shiny, and equipped with all the latest gadgets. In our pasture right behind the barn, there is a protected area that's great for feeding cattle, except in one place—the quicksand spot. It's roughly forty feet in diameter. A crowbar thrown in the middle will disappear in a short time. In summer you can avoid it because you can see it. In winter it freezes hard, and you can drive over it, making it easier to feed the cattle.

That December the temperature crept above freezing and remained there for a few days. On a Sunday morning, Dad climbed into his shiny new tractor to quickly feed the cattle before heading into town for church. In short order, hay filled most of the troughs. It looked like he'd get to church on time. He maneuvered the tractor to pick up the last load, then shifted gears to drive the tractor forward. Nothing happened. Dad glanced back. What he saw was the back end of the tractor sinking into the quicksand ... all the way to the top of the back tires.

What do you do when the back end of your new John Deere is completely submerged in a thawing sinkhole?

Many would have given up on that tractor. That's the unforgiving nature of quicksand. Not my dad. He remained optimistic that there had to be a solution for getting his brand-new tractor back to work. He quickly dove into problem-solving mode.

The tractor had stopped sinking, so for days after, he searched and eventually found a man experienced in dragging oil tankers and semitrucks out of precarious situations. It was expensive, but Dad's optimism prevailed and he saved the tractor.

What lesson did I learn from him? That being stuck, literally or figuratively, is no match for one's mental strength and external resources. His attitude toward adversity was one of realistic optimism. He had a hopefulness and confidence that got him through many difficult situations.

Optimism is a confident belief, or mind-set, that expects good outcomes even when facing tough circumstances. It requires active virtues of faith, hope, temperance, and prudence.

Who exemplified realistic optimism for you during your growing-up years?

Millennials and Optimism

This "stuck tractor" level of tenacity and optimism for solving problems needs to be developed and nurtured in our next-gen leaders. Eighty percent of millennials think they'll be as well or better off than their parents. But more than half are still living paycheck to paycheck, and 35 percent are getting financial help from their families, according to a 2014 Bank of America/*USA Today* Better Money Habits Millennial Report.[1]

Despite millennials' seemingly negative financial situation, other studies agree that these young people appear to be, in general, more optimistic about the future than their parents are. When I talk with members of this generation, I'm sometimes amazed at the carefree attitude some of them have about either finding employment or resigning from a job. They don't seem to think they should be working hard to climb the ranks, and they don't seem to attach a stigma to being laid off or fired, like our generation did.

A WORD FROM A MILLENNIAL ...

"We often assume that we can *always* find something better."

This natural optimism provides the perfect opportunity for experienced leaders to support mentees in a constructive way. I'm a firm believer in the Pygmalion effect, which suggests that higher expectations lead to an increase in performance.

It can be easy for some to get discouraged by all the uncontrollable issues in our world, such as terrorism, debt, global warming, and a rocky political landscape. However, by focusing their attention, and ours, on what we *can* control, we will move forward with realistic optimism, the kind I witnessed in my dad's attitude toward the stuck tractor.

How to Nurture Optimism
in Your Next-Gen Leader

High morale is usually tied to increased creativity, critical thinking, decision making, and productivity. This is not a rose-tinted-glasses brand of optimism. "Don't worry, be happy" doesn't quite cut it. A true optimist is aware of the issues at hand and yet makes a deliberate choice to stay positive.

Be willing to share some tips and strategies from your personal experience that have helped you overcome daunting discouragements. Here are some of the optimistic insights I've learned.

See Humor in Life

I love what the ancient sage Solomon says, "A cheerful heart is good medicine, but a broken spirit saps a person's strength"

(Proverbs 17:22 NLT). Show your own ability to find humor, even in the midst of a tense and difficult situation. Teach your young leader how humor breaks the tension in stressful situations and, if used correctly, builds their leadership quotient.

Cultivate Gratitude

When your next-gen leader is stuck, either literally or figuratively, it's easy to focus on what's disheartening and discouraging. Everything seems to have a gray hue. However, the attitude of being grateful is completely separate from our circumstance. One can change their entire life by cultivating a grateful outlook. That may sound a bit dramatic, but recent brain chemistry research, which David D. Burns discusses in *Feeling Good: The New Mood Therapy*, confirms that the more exercise you give your brain in being grateful, the more you can defeat hopelessness and be more spontaneously grateful in the future. Gratefulness turns on the light switch, shedding light on possible solutions.[2]

So how do you cultivate gratefulness? Here are a few ideas to share with your mentee:

- Have them carry a gratitude journal, and commit to recording at least three things in the journal throughout the day.
- If there's someone your young leader isn't getting along with, urge them to write three to five positive attributes they notice in that person during the day. Depending on how cantankerous the relationship is, this may take a long time to do, but the payoff of rewiring their brain is worth it.
- Have them record ten items or situations they're grateful for at the end of each day. They'll get uplifting food-for-thought in their brain before falling asleep.

Focus on the Truth

Does your next-gen leader know the acronym FEAR—False Evidence Appearing Real? In today's world, it can be easy to get all worked up by "fake news," whether it pertains to politics, angst from prospects or clients, or talk at the water cooler. Discuss with your mentee times you learned the hard way to focus on the truth. You'll build optimism as well as perspective. Dwell on the known facts. If you want to know what's in the future, you have to start by focusing on today's facts.

Hang with the Right Crowd

Remind your mentee to surround himself or herself with optimistic people at work who energize others, and to limit their time with pessimistic, draining people. This will stimulate creativity and increase job satisfaction. Feel free to share a time when you learned this the hard way. Also, strive to model it now that you're more seasoned.

Ask for Help

Remind your young leader to reach out for help. The conditions we face are often beyond the scope of our abilities, but not beyond the scope of our community or our Creator, God.

A WORD FROM A MILLENNIAL …

"Prayer helps too. I'm not certain how many of your readers are comfortable with prayer, but I have personally experienced prayer as a key source of optimism."

My dad's worst stuck-tractor experience happened ages ago, but when I asked him about it, he immediately recalled the facts. Surely this experience had a huge impact on him since he could remember it so vividly many years later.

I believe that it was my dad's ability to always be optimistic—to expect a good outcome in a bad situation—that propelled him into problem-solving mode on that Sunday morning. We have the opportunity to instill this powerful character trait in our young leaders, a deliberate choice to expect a good outcome, no matter the severity of the issues they face.

A WORD FROM A MILLENNIAL ...

"I'm not so sure how many millennials believe that hard work and perseverance pay off. I think many of us grew up with unhappy workaholic parents. We don't want that for ourselves. Many of us have jobs where we don't see the value in our work. It makes us want to work hard for forty hours per week, but then go focus on 'more meaningful things.'"

LEADERSHIP LESSON

Optimism is an activating force.
It invigorates us when we face overwhelming
obstacles. It helps us envision a promising
future and pursue compelling goals.

Trustworthiness: Leading with Compelling Integrity

How much value do you place on trustworthiness?

My go-to expert on trust, in any business climate, is speaker and best-selling author David Horsager. I know David personally, and he is a person who lives what he talks about. This word of wisdom from his book *The Trust Edge* is relevant to our conversation: "The single uniqueness of the greatest leaders and organizations of all time is trust."[1]

Sometimes we find that prominent leaders set high standards for others but aren't trustworthy themselves when faced with moral or ethical dilemmas. Some of it makes the news wires, and some of it happens out of the limelight.

David Horsager makes the case for the importance of trust in our daily personal and professional lives. Here's a short summary of what I've learned from his material in *The Trust Edge* and through reading his excellent articles and newsletters:

- Trust, or a lack of it, has the ability to accelerate or destroy any business, organization, or relationship.
- People follow the trusted leader. They buy from the trusted salesperson. For the trusted brand, people will pay more, come back, and tell others.
- One of the biggest driving forces of trust is the perception that someone is concerned beyond themselves for the good of the whole. Firefighters and nurses care for others by nature of their jobs. But we wonder if the salesperson really has our best interests in mind.

- Never mind the general untrustworthiness of your industry. Decide to be among the trusted in your field.

A WORD FROM A MILLENNIAL...

"Be the one who starts raising the bar little by little. Set a new standard at your office, and you may see a new standard for your profession in the community, region, or country."

Millennials and Trustworthiness

Horsager's message is resonating around the globe, from Main Street to Wall Street. We've all experienced breaches of trust in many of the institutions we used to admire. In fact, trust in most institutions currently ranks close to an all-time low in our nation.

Millennials have been particularly wounded, since many trust scandals hit during their impressionable years. As a consequence, they're slow to trust. Look at these results of a recent poll by Harvard University's Institute of Politics:

- 88 percent only sometimes or never trust the press
- 86 percent distrust Wall Street
- 82 percent distrust Congress
- 74 percent don't trust the federal government to do what's right
- 63 percent lack trust that the president will make the right decisions
- 58 percent aren't convinced the Supreme Court makes good decisions[2]

While trust in institutions and government is falling, the trust placed in complete strangers is growing like bread dough. Take the rise of Uber, Zipcar, and Airbnb,[3] for example. They're enjoying incredible success.

It seems that the deck is stacked against us as leaders, that it's close to impossible to earn the trust of this next generation of young professionals. Their willingness to hear us as leaders depends on whether or not we've earned their trust and respect. Then, and only then, can we mentor them on the importance of high integrity.

How to Grow a Trustworthy Character in Your Next-Gen Leader

Albert Einstein said, "Whoever is careless with the truth in small matters cannot be trusted in important affairs." So, how can you help your upcoming leader to grow their leadership capacity and value, for both themselves and your company?

Conduct a Trusted Advisor Survey

When I coach any given salesperson on how to be a trusted resource instead of just another irritating salesperson, I show them these characteristics of a trusted resource, which are adapted from *The Trusted Advisor*,[4] by Maister, Green, and Galford. I ask my coaching clients to rate themselves on a scale of 1 to 10 (10 being the highest). We don't know if they are trusted until they score 10s.

As a trusted person, you:

- Are consistent and dependable
- Can be relied on to tell clients the truth
- Are on the clients' side and always seem to have their best interests at heart
- Are always honorable in words and actions
- Act like a real person, not someone in a role
- Allow clients and colleagues latitude to think; you don't just give your conclusions
- Double check people's assumptions to help them uncover false assumptions

- Are motivated to always do the right thing
- Are constantly finding new ways to be of greater service
- Are committed to doing the next right thing

Next, we strategize how to leverage the 10s to meet their goals. We then evaluate where they scored less than 10 and prioritize which characteristics they want to strengthen. Then we develop a plan that includes concrete actions where they can measure their success. It's important to talk through what behaviors they are going to do differently. Otherwise it's just talk, no action. And if there's no action, results will stay the same.

Improve Sales Posturing

Becoming a trusted resource is a competitive advantage in today's hyper-competitive business climate. Sales professionals whom prospects and clients trust naturally differentiate themselves from the competitors quickly. A salesperson who earns the reputation of being a trusted resource is able to uncover the root problem through deep discovery, which involves extensive questioning and listening. Based on this understanding of the real need(s) to address, they're able to help chart a product and/ or service solution that is good for their client in the long run. They're always thinking in terms of win-win relationships—that is, what's good for the company and what's good for the client.

Grow Leadership Influence

You can also use David Horsager's model as a coaching and mentoring guide in the area of trust, using the 1-to-10 survey model. Those eight pillars are clarity, compassion, character, contribution, competency, connection, commitment, and consistency.

Both leadership and sales teams are rooted in the dedication to helping others solve problems. Teaching next-gen leaders the long-term value of trust is imperative. It cannot be built overnight, but must be earned over time by demonstrating that your daily actions, both personally and professionally, align with your words.

The reality of this broken world is that we will encounter lies and dishonesty. It'll be no different for the next generation of leaders and the generation after that. So it's crucial that we, as experienced leaders, model trustworthiness as well as teach our mentees the importance of being trusted resources for clients and colleagues. Trustworthiness comes when you are worthy of being trusted by others, especially when facing moral and ethical predicaments. This trust is built on the virtues of justice, fortitude, temperance, and love.

LEADERSHIP LESSON

Cultivating a courageous character core requires trustworthiness. Trustworthiness and truthfulness must be demonstrated for and nurtured in young leaders.

8

Accountability: Answerability Advances Courage

"I can't help it ... It was his fault ... She made me do it." From the elementary school to the corner office, these words are spoken by people who don't want to take responsibility. Victim mode doesn't go far with me, or with any other experienced leader I know.

In my work, I help company presidents and CEOs improve their sales teams' productivity. It's not uncommon for me to step in and have to deal with blame-gaming toxicity. It's like a cancer. The list of whom or what to blame is endless. I hear about the uncooperative economy, tight marketplace, stiff competition, incompetent colleague, and the bad boss. I hear blame directed at the marketing department or the production team. I also find that people who tend to pass blame do so out of years of habit.

There's no way a company, a team, or an individual can have full access to their innovation and productivity when they aren't taking personal responsibility for their actions and behaviors. In contrast, accountable up-and-coming leaders will ask, "What might *I* do to help solve the problem?" Excuse-busting questions like this, when used over time, develop high individual performance and a positive, energizing culture.

Accountability means having the emotional maturity and internal backbone to take responsibility for your own actions and choices, and not shift blame to external factors. Accountability is an expression of the virtues of fortitude, prudence, justice, temperance, and faith.

Millennials and Accountability

One of the biggest negative character traits continually linked to millennials is their sense of entitlement, the feeling that they deserve to be given something. Many millennials do exceedingly well at the blame game.

And like with every other generation, there are millennials who defy this stereotype. Those who do have been avid learners of our victim-oriented culture. We've all read about the lawsuits against McDonald's for making the coffee too hot or for causing someone's obesity.

I get a kick out of reading excuses that employees come up with for being late for work. Here are three comical entries I read recently while skimming the Internet[1]:

1. I forgot it wasn't the weekend.
2. The sunrise was so beautiful that I had to stop and take it in.
3. My mother-in-law wouldn't stop talking.

These are funny excuses, but coaching and mentoring millennials in our blame-game world is an important responsibility. As experienced leaders, we need to be proactive in addressing this lack of accountability. It will take persistent finesse on our part to navigate these conversations.

How to Foster Accountability in Your Next-Gen Leader

In *The Advantage,* Patrick Lencioni shares this powerful truth about accountability: "To hold someone accountable is to care about them enough to risk having them blame you for pointing out their deficiencies."[2]

In some circles, "accountability" has become a code word for "find someone to blame." We like to talk about how "someone should be held accountable for this." However, a leader who is truly accountable will find creative solutions to minimize the damage and fix the problem.

It's often countercultural to have the humility and confidence to acknowledge that we're solely responsible for 1) the choices we make in our lives and 2) whatever it is we choose to think and feel. Accountability is well worth modeling to emerging leaders. If they don't see you navigate your way through rocky situations, they won't learn accountability from you. In watching you, a young leader experiences personal and professional growth, propelling them forward in the leadership journey.

Lencioni's perspective gives us fresh insight on our leadership and mentoring role, as well as how to guide others.

Listen Critically

Suggest that your mentee listen honestly to their own self-talk.

- Do they shift blame when they make a mistake or perform poorly?
- When do they choose to blame others?
- Do they have someone who is their go-to option for blaming?
- Or, do they blame a situation that occurred in their past as the culprit?
- What are the patterns?

We all go through times when it feels easier to blame someone or something, rather than exercise our personal choice to act versus just react. The best place to start developing good accountability skills is to be honest with yourself.

I often find that my instinctive reaction is to externalize. Then, after I reflect on the situation for one or two days and my emotions subside, I begin to see what I might do differently to get a more preferential outcome.

This will be hard, introspective work for your mentee. You can be a supportive guide along the way. As you work together, you may be surprised to discover some hidden excuses of choice of your own. Admit them. Then commit to shifting your mind-set.

A WORD FROM A MILLENNIAL …

"Be around people who have high expectations of themselves. It's hard to keep raising the bar for yourself when everyone else in your circle is ready and willing to sit back and cast blame."

Learn the Serenity Prayer

You might be familiar with the famous and often-quoted Serenity Prayer. It reminds us what we are accountable for:

> *God, grant me the serenity to accept*
> *the things I cannot change,*
> *courage to change the things I can,*
> *and wisdom to know the difference.*

Share stories with your mentee about when you've had to shift gears and take a wiser stance.

Carry a Round Tuit

Did you every carry one of these in your pocket or purse when you were growing up? I think my parents gave mine to me as a gift when I was a teenager. Evidently I hadn't been getting my regular chores done.

This was inscribed on my Round Tuit: "This is a round tuit. Guard it with your life! Tuits are hard to come by, especially the round ones. It will help you become a much more efficient worker. For years you've heard people say, 'I'll do that when I get a round tuit.' So now that you have one, you can accomplish all those things you put aside until you got a Round Tuit."

It's been a great gift, a reminder to hold myself accountable to my commitments. Perhaps your mentee needs this gift also.

Focus on Positive Action Instead of Reaction

"What you do when you don't have to, will determine what you will do when you can't help it." As a young salesperson, I posted this quote everywhere—on my bathroom mirror, inside my planner, in my briefcase, and by my nightstand. It's about accountability, isn't it?

Your next-gen leader doesn't have to examine their own contributions to a negative situation. They don't have to accept responsibility for the poor choices they're making with their life. They don't have to take ownership of how they're choosing to think and feel about a situation. However, by doing so, they build their internal leadership capacity so that when they're in a difficult spot, they'll be able to stimulate others to choose well.

Invite your young leader to embrace an excuse-free character core. This mind-set minimizes excuses and maximizes the search for creative solutions, which is vital during times of chaos and conflict. In our "the coffee is too hot" culture, we need to go the extra mile to be aware of the crippling impact of playing the victim role. Our leadership legacy is enhanced when we guide young leaders to not only accept accountability but also seek it out.

LEADERSHIP LESSON

Accountability, coupled with a resolve
to find creative solutions, yields strong character.

Dear Reader,

You've been given a gift. Many people of strong character invested in you. They coached and mentored you relationally, physically, intellectually, spiritually, and financially. This gift to you has impacted every role and responsibility you've undertaken on your leadership journey. Their gift gave you the character core that allows you to have firm footing, so that you can have positive influence at home, in your business, and with your stakeholders.

It's your turn to pass this gift along to your next-gen leader. Now that's sustainable leadership, part of your legacy.

> *Keep vigilant watch over your heart;*
> *that's where life starts.*
> PROVERBS 4:23

The heart is where life—and leadership—starts.

—Danita

An Interview with Brandon Schaefer, Executive Director of Five Capitals

As business owners, we make decisions every day related to our financial capital, strength, and resources. Of course, we wrestle with relationship capital also—that is, hiring, training, retaining, and firing personnel, especially when it impacts the movement of the trend line of our financial capital.

My curiosity was immediately piqued when I heard Brandon talking about the importance of stewarding all five capitals or resources within our care. I wondered, *Five? What are the five?*

In every interaction with Brandon and the Five Capital's team, I am invited to live more intentionally and purposefully in all areas of life.

Q: What's your vision for Five Capitals, Brandon?

Brandon: Our vision is to be the best in the world at helping business leaders discover (and live out) a life of impact and purpose (John 10:10). We accomplish this through investing in the areas of professional development (self-awareness), leadership skills (influencing others), and organizational strategy (industry best practices). Our coaches are expert practitioners in meeting leaders where they are, discerning the best path forward, and then helping them achieve their goals. We have a solid track record to seeing marketplace leaders (and their businesses) get to the greater levels of success and significance for which they are looking.

Q: As you're working with business owners and leaders, what are their challenges with millennials?

Brandon: The first is finding and retaining good talent. It's always hard to find strong talent, but especially today. Younger leaders want companies they believe in. They look for companies to fuel their passion. You can no longer sell vacation time, salary, and bonus checks. You have to have your vision and values in order, set people up for success, and provide opportunities to engage their passions.

Q: What else are you seeing, Brandon?

Brandon: Number two is that people are really challenged by how marketing has changed. Traditional marketing models no longer work, and business owners are struggling to figure out new growth strategies, whether it's social media or relation-based selling. It's difficult to adjust to these new marketing methods and vehicles.

Q: How are you seeing these market forces impact selling strategies?

Brandon: Selling strategies aren't as transactional as they used to be. Relational capital is the new currency. It's about building trust, developing relationships, and setting ourselves apart from competitors. Cultivating trust and relationships based on character is critical. Thus, the selling cycle is slower.

Q: You've developed the concept of the Five Capitals. How do you see these impacting businesses?

Brandon: In 2005, the book *Freakonomics* by Steven Levitt intrigued us. It talks about all the types of capital in world economies and the complexity of selling in the global market. That got us thinking: How do we boil down all these different types of capital, both personally and professionally? Then, how do we order them in a way that people and their organizations find the most success, as well as the most fulfillment? What we have found with our research and engagement with thousands of clients is that you can condense all the different types of capital into five categories. We also found an order to those capitals that sets someone up for the most success.

Q: Can you tell me about the Five Capitals and a little bit about why each of them is important?

Brandon: First and foremost is Spiritual Capital. It's about your connection and relationship with God. Everyone has to wrestle with the faith component. Spiritual Capital has the power to create incredible levels of identity and security in understanding your values. It clarifies who you are, defines your values, and reveals the good you want to bring the world. When Spiritual Capital is the center of your life and you lead from that place, phenomenal things happen in terms of health, productivity, and service.

The second is really about love of people. Relational Capital is all about the health and productivity of our relationships. It's about trust, engagement, and integrity. It's about being a leader who is worth following.

The third one is Physical Capital. All of us have only

one life in this world. Time is the great equalizer. No matter if you're serving as president, finishing college, starting a second career, or working as a tenured employee, we all have the same twenty-four hours each day.

Intellectual Capital is next. All wisdom comes from God. We need to continually gain insight, tools, wisdom, and creativity. Discernment for the best path forward, whether it is prioritizing our day or determining how to launch a new product, comes from experience.

And the fifth capital is Financial Capital. It is being a good steward of all the resources in our organization's possession. It's focusing on managing profitability and revenue well, which creates the opportunity to use that capital for good.

Q: This all sounds so wonderfully intuitive, Brandon. What's the catch?

Brandon: Great question! The catch is most people don't put the capitals in this order. This keeps them from high levels of fulfillment and productivity. For example, the boomers tend to put Financial Capital first. It's all about the bottom line, and then comes Intellectual Capital. How can I be smart and well known so I can get promoted and make more money? Physically, most of the boomers work too hard and burn out or end up blowing up the organization. Finally, they tend to use and abuse relationships, while often neglecting the most important relationships—spouse, kids, and God.

Q: How do you find millennials respond to this model?

Brandon: Millennials experienced this mis-ordering of capitals firsthand from their parents, aunts and uncles, and other older leaders. They've observed that it doesn't produce the life they want, so they often put the capitals in a different order.

Q: What order do you see this generation prioritizing?

Brandon: First and foremost, millennials prioritize their Relational Capital. While they want a healthy life and a path to expressing their passions, those are not as big of a deal for millennials as relationships. Technology has made Intellectual Capital readily available and easier to achieve. It's right there on their smartphone, day and night. Finally, Financial Capital is a much lower priority with millennials than with older generations. They simply are not as motivated by money as they are by people and other intangibles.

Q: This must create a conflict in the workplace since nearly every company has multiple generations working together?

Brandon: It creates incredible tension. Priorities, focus, and values are different. These differences lead to disconnection between millennials and their older leaders. So a re-orientation by both generations needs to take place to understand where each is coming from.

Q: Insightful. So for a business owner or a business leader who's committed to raising up this next generation of leaders in millennials, what are some of your recommendations?

Brandon: Foremost, get your vision and values in order. When I worked for Motorola, we had all these slogans about putting the customer first, courtesy, hard work, and our vision. But everyone knew the priority was quarterly earnings statements and annual results. Millennials can sniff that out so fast. Leaders need compelling and inspiring brand, vision, and values that aren't just on the wall, but are actually lived out. Millennials want to be part of something impactful.

Q: What else is important for leaders to consider when thinking about the Five Capitals?

Brandon: Think relational, not transactional. It's important to develop a great relationship with younger leaders. They want to understand what makes you tick, your passions, and what is important to your heart. They also want you to know the same about them. Create space to connect with people through coffee meetings or getting families together. Building trust and relationship with young leaders will come back to you in plenty with buy-in, commitment, productivity, and a desire to see your vision continue.

Q: Relational Capital rules in today's world. Any other important things that are helpful to know about this new generation of leaders?

Brandon: Be sure to demonstrate a pathway for greater opportunities. Not just financial or promotional, but ones that make a difference in the organization. Lastly, understand you'll have to make space for extracurricular activities. Millennials want to be out the door by five so they can engage in their hobbies and interests or meet up with friends. They need their employer, given they work hard, to support what they do outside of work.

Q: I'm including a Five Capitals overview in the appendix, both an overview that includes a fuller definition of each of the five wealths we have to steward, plus Building Trust—how relational capital can help you better serve your customers. Where else can we go?

Brandon: At FiveCapitals.net we have a number of helpful resources. While you're there, sign up to get my blog posting. When we connect, make certain to let me know that we connected through Danita and *Millennials Matter*.

Unless a man is master of his soul,
all other kinds of mastery
amount to little.

—Teddy Roosevelt

Part 2

Practice
Proactive Self-Care

Definition: A personal initiative that prioritizes
developing depth of well-being so that
character grows in influence.

9

Proactive Self-Care
and Leadership

In 1987, my husband, Gordon, and I moved to St. Cloud, Minnesota. We decided to build a house on eleven acres that fronted the Mississippi River, and acted as our own general contractor, which was quite a learning adventure for two novices in construction. During this time, our first daughter was born.

The never-ending decisions of the building project, my pressure-cooker work schedule, and my best motherhood intentions led to incessant guilt. When I was at work, I felt guilty for not being with my daughter and helping Gordon with the building project. When I was at home, I felt distracted by what I left at work.

I tried to present a brave face to the outside world, but one morning I burst into tears. The move into our new house was being delayed by a month. This meant we were going to be bringing our newborn baby home to a tiny no-star motel room. The tears wouldn't quit.

My typical mode of action wasn't working. Tackling the next urgent item on my to-do list wasn't enough. I realized I was so focused on checking things off my list that I was oblivious to what was happening in my inner world. To move forward from this moment and live life more intentionally, I needed to listen much more deeply and strategically to myself.

In launching this new approach of paying attention to and prioritizing my entire self—meaning relationally, physically, intellectually, spiritually, and financially—I had embarked on a personal listening initiative to build a more robust root system where I could stand firm.

Proactive self-care is a personal initiative that prioritizes developing a depth of wellness that fosters character growth and expands influence. Becoming so much more aware of my goals and instincts has helped me to prioritize raising strong future leaders and building a career that influences the world in a positive way.

Being Proactive and Prioritizing Self-Awareness

One of the characteristics I've noticed in leaders who've modeled strong moral and character leadership over a lifetime is that they pay acute attention to what's happening in their internal world. This self-awareness and self-care extends to all areas of their lives.

Their passion for growth is evident to all as they maintain a steadfast attention to their core values. They exude a humble confidence in all situations. They take a learning stance on their self-improvement efforts and are able to receive criticism and turn it into constructive action. In the midst of a stressful, high-speed culture, they still prioritize time to listen to themselves, to listen to God, and to disconnect from the constant pressures of the world. From this intentional space and quiet place, they gain internal strength and stability. It is from a similar place that we find the capacity to raise up other leaders.

In the semiarid Northern Plains, trees are revered. There are so few of them that you're in awe when you see them in contrast to the fields of wheat and prairie grasses. You wonder, *How can they even grow? Yes, they're sun-soaked, but where do they get the water and the nutrients?*

It's all in the roots. A healthy root system is vital to a tree's survival. The roots actively seek out the water, oxygen, and nutrients needed for a tree to grow, be stable enough to withstand tornado-force winds, and reproduce with seeds and fruit. None of this happens without an active root system.

The same is true for us. Our character is the root system that feeds our capacity to grow. Leaders take intentional, proactive, thoughtful care of their roots.

A WORD FROM A MILLENNIAL ...

"There are two ancient Scriptures I often read together. First, I love King David's imagery of being a tree planted by streams of water that yields fruit in every season and has leaves that do not wither (Psalm 1:3). Then, I think of Paul when he prays that followers of Jesus would be rooted and grounded in love (Ephesians 3:17). In my mind's eye, I see a tree that's vibrant and flourishing above the ground because of a massive root system that is tapped into God's love and wisdom."

In contrast to wise, proactive leaders, there are leaders who eventually topple because they focus too much on one, or a few, priorities. They may appear successful initially, but eventually the winds of life blow them over. Personal or work relationships might be damaged, or they might struggle with physical or emotional burnout. Though they seem to press forward without incident, it's unsustainable. Eventually the neglected area of life falls apart, and everyone and everything around them gets caught in the wreckage.

There's another trap I've seen some leaders fall prey to. They know that all areas of life are important. They may even go to a life-planning retreat and map out their ideal, balanced self-care needs. However, they don't develop the disciplines and practices to execute their lofty plans. Thus, their leadership style fails to bring about their good intentions.

One of the more frustrating leadership development projects I've ever faced was working with a person who had zero motivation to be proactive and was grossly unaware of the importance of holistic self-care. It remains a mystery to me how this man was promoted to a leadership position in the first place. When I met him, he appeared to be hopping from one crisis to another, trying to put out fires as they started. He relied heavily on the opinions and wishes of others to guide his leadership, but that meant he was swaying like a reed in the wind. His next move was determined by whomever he would speak with right before he made the decision.

A WORD FROM A MILLENNIAL …

"A colleague told me of a manager she had who was reading a new leadership book every month. Each month, he'd roll out a new mantra, new approach, new framework—a new something to the staff. They never took it seriously, writing it off as merely the 'flavor of the month.' Although a lot of the ideas were probably great, none could take root because of how they were presented."

How can you help your millennials to reach an intentional, quiet space where they can discover their internal strength to flourish? How can you teach them proactive self-care?

Your Next-Gen Leader and Proactive Self-Care

For millennials, the scenarios are different but the difficulty is the same. The external milieu relentlessly demands their attention. During conversations with emerging leaders, they often confess the following:

- "My heart races when I realize I forgot my phone at home or left it in the other room."
- "Sometimes social media distracts me from getting my job done."
- "Occasionally I feel lonely even though I've been with people all day."
- "I sometimes wake up tired. It could be from my phone beeping all night long."

For many, a technology detox is needed in order to reset priorities and learn how to listen. This is one of the reasons that yoga and meditation are mainstream with both men and women. Yes, health is important to millennials. Almost all the young leaders I know prioritize exercising and eating well. But it's their desire to practice the art of mindfulness while unwinding and de-stressing that is most interesting. They can unplug faster than any other generation.

Let's be honest. Yoga and meditation practices are not enough to build a strong root system for sustainable leadership to flourish. They're great components to self-care, but limited. Without a strong and wide root system, we end up stressed, burned out, and exhausted. Then it's difficult, if not impossible, to do any business wisely.

This is where you can help your next-gen leader. Many of the character concerns raised by the 271 business leaders, CEOs, presidents, and business advisors we surveyed were issues that are only addressed through introspective work.

A WORD FROM A MILLENNIAL ...

"There seems to be such a push for self-care that you are almost looked down upon if you don't ignore others to put yourself first. Those in my life that boast about having 'self-care' figured out seem nothing but selfish to me."

How do you proactively mentor next-gen sales and business leaders on the practice of proactive self-care? From personal experience (and failure), I know this is an essential habit for young leaders to start developing before they burn out. Nurturing healthy personal and professional lives is foundational for gaining leadership traction. It's not just about how efficient we are in our jobs, but also whether we are exercising sound judgment and discernment.

The advancement of self-care involves numerous disciplines, including breaking the chains of negative thinking, dealing with their dark side, setting goals, and developing a healthy work-rest rhythm.

It was in that tiny, no-star motel room that I first learned that no matter how much the outside world demands, it's paramount to take care of your inner being. When we're healthy physically and mentally, it becomes easier to balance and prioritize our work and personal lives.

Proactive self-care will enable your next-gen leader to resolve feelings of conflict and become a leader of character who can deal with and grow from any setback.

LEADERSHIP LESSON

Taking proactive care of your inner self
strengthens your personal being. Then you
will thrive, even in the most volatile times.

10

Break the Chains of Negative Thinking

On December 3, 2005, I felt devastated. The four big deals that I *knew* would close didn't. All four prospects informed me of their no-go decision on the same day.

How could I have been so wrong about all four deals? I told myself, *Throw in the towel, Danita. Give up. Find something you're remotely competent at.*

Have you ever felt that way? Like everything you thought was the right thing to do, is no longer getting you the same results?

Our Christmas break ski vacation sounded like a great place to forget about it all and start the year fresh. I couldn't wait to catch up on some reading. You'd think I would have picked a more uplifting title than John Eldredge's *Waking the Dead*, but the subtitle, "The Glory of a Heart Fully Alive," showed promise. Yes, that's what I needed.

I read the first few sentences of the book and realized I was about to have my internal world exposed.

Eldredge suggested that one way to take responsibility for your emotional and spiritual well-being is to become more aware of your thoughts. This came at a good time for me. I wrote a list of all the unsupportive things I believed about myself:

- I'm a rotten salesperson (Who gets four nos in one day? Then, I let it get personal.).
- I'm too short.
- I'm not smart.
- I'm not funny.

Before long I had seven pages packed with life-sucking lies. My strongholds of pride and fear were giving way to low self-esteem. I measured myself against others and let people's outward appearance and position influence me. I was a sapling in the wind.

What has been your leadership progression in this regard? How have you dealt with your internal critic?

Millennials and Negative Self-Talk

If I allowed discouraging thoughts into my belief system, then other people, including millennials, surely struggle with unsupportive thoughts as well. Millennials are often labeled as narcissistic know-it-alls, but in my experience, they often suffer from invalidating thinking and low self-esteem. They constantly measure themselves against others.

Beware. Mentors must not be fooled by what is really just a form of overcompensating. People who struggle the most might have the best-looking Instagram accounts. Our social-media-saturated culture measures "success" by the number of likes, comments, or shares.

A low performance fuels their negative self-talk. It's counterproductive, leading to increased stress levels and possible depression.

That's why experienced leaders need to be attentive to negative self-talk in their mentees. Young leaders may look and sound confident, but in reality we're all human and have areas where we can become healthier in our thinking. These findings from the University of California Davis Undergraduate Executive Summary Spring 2015, affirm the need for our vigilance:

Over the previous twelve months:

- 24 percent felt things were hopeless;
- 17.5 percent felt overwhelmed by what they had to do;
- 25.4 percent felt very lonely; and

- 20 percent felt so depressed that it was difficult to function.[1]

There is never a fast track to leadership development. It's a long-term growth and maturity process that stems from a healthy root structure.

Work with Your Next-Gen Leader to Break the Chains

Unsupportive thoughts hide in our subconscious minds and wield power over our everyday lives. In my coaching, I help sales professionals and leaders replace their negative self-talk with supportive self-talk. We often work on improving sales capacity, and we deal with issues such as these:

- Fighting the need for approval
- Counteracting low self-esteem
- Minimizing the discomfort of talking about money
- Learning to control emotions in the moment
- Developing a closing instinct
- Conquering call reluctance

Addressing these mind-sets has a dramatic impact on the leadership and sales performance of your next-gen leader. Through mentoring, we ultimately help them strengthen their overall life skills and develop healthy thinking habits.

Identify Negative Thinking Patterns

Sometimes it can be difficult for any of us, including the person you're coaching, to identify negative beliefs. I have a validated survey process I use in my consulting to help me quickly identify hidden mind-set weaknesses in salespeople, sales teams, and leaders. However, when sitting down over a cup of coffee in a more casual setting, I invite the young leaders to complete the questions below. Their responses give added insight into what is going on beneath the surface. I tell them to answer with their first instinct.

This might be a useful exercise for you to do with your mentee. You might both be surprised by your own answers. Fill in the blanks in the following statements:

- I would be more effective if I wasn't so _____.
- I would achieve more if I didn't have to deal with _____.
- I'm afraid to _____.
- I'm not inspired enough to _____.
- I can't _____.

Usually people are shocked by their instinctive responses. If they don't like their own answers, invite them to walk through the following three-step process to help them install truths that can take control of their thoughts. It will help them achieve their goals and dreams.

Recognize the Destructive Impact of Negative Thinking

Invite your mentee to write down some of the consequences they've experienced as a result of destructive thought patterns. Viewing the consequences of these untruths on paper can be shocking. Work through this together. When a thought is deeply rooted in our psyche, it can be difficult to see how destructive it is without bringing it out into the open to analyze. Talk through the adverse effects that this damaging belief has on their identity, relationships, influence, and life goals.

Destroy the Lies

For many it can be helpful to do a conscious and physical action to demonstrate to our unconscious internal self that we have made a concrete decision to destroy the falsehoods and their control over our lives. Ask your young leader what physical demonstration they would like to do. Rip their unsupportive thoughts apart, literally, by ripping the papers into pieces? Burn them? Flush them? It's a physical reminder that the negative cycle of these thoughts has been broken and no longer has control.

A WORD FROM A MILLENNIAL ...

"Or invite them to find another way that helps them *know* and *feel* that they are actively destroying the lies that most haunt them. They could stomp on the paper or feed it to the shredder, for example."

Install Truth

Complete this powerful process by having your mentee write truth statements that counteract the lies that were just destroyed. Have them use the following guidelines as they pen their truth statements.

- Be sure the affirmations are short so they're easier to remember.
- Personalize each statement by starting with "I" or "My."
- Write them all in present tense.

A WORD FROM A MILLENNIAL ...

"In my life, calling a lie what it is—a lie—and then rejecting it takes a lot of bravery. We almost become more comfortable with the lie than we do with the idea of looking through the lens of truth. This is not easy."

Review Truth Regularly

Encourage your next-gen leader to keep their truth affirmations nearby and review them regularly. Lies are deeply engrained in our neural pathways. That's why it takes deliberate, conscious, and persistent repetition to rewire our thinking.

I have my truth statements written out where I can see them and also recorded in my voice memos on my phone. So whether I'm exercising, driving, or waiting at the doctor's office, I can review them.

Others I work with keep their affirmations on sticky notes at home, on their bathroom mirrors, or at their computer desks. Many would prefer to have them on their phones or perhaps even as tattoos. Diligence is necessary to wipe out those old negative ideas that try to sneak back into our thought patterns.

Our thoughts drive our behavior, and our behavior dictates our accomplishments. Here's what's most amazing: We have the power to decide that unsupportive thoughts are not allowed to control our lives; we can choose what nutrients we feed our root systems.

Help your future leader to break the power of these negative thinking patterns today so they will know that one lost deal (or four) doesn't mean they have to feel devastated, throw in the towel, or give up on their dreams.

LEADERSHIP LESSON

Watch your thoughts.
Be aware of negative self-talk.

11

Deal with Your Dark Side

Keep vigilant watch over your heart;
that's where life starts.
PROVERBS 4:23

As a young country girl, I lived in paradise. We had a huge backyard, lots of cattle, hills to climb, and rugged coulees to play hide-and-seek. We also had abundant reading material in the form of two sets of encyclopedias. One set actually included black and white pictures. Plus, my favorite, the *National Geographic*, was packed with exotic, colorful photographs of far-away places. And—lucky me!—I got to take a Finnish sauna every Saturday evening. This was paradise for any young child.

Paradise got shattered in first grade when I met the city girls at school. I was different. A misfit. I was the country girl, the girl from the "other side of the tracks." I had no TV to watch the cartoons that the kids talked about. I had no flushing toilet at home. And people thought the sauna weird. Recess confirmed my insecurities when I was the last one to be picked for the kickball team. I began to think I was a loser.

To protect my sensitive heart from further humiliation, I stopped participating in games or events where there was a chance I'd be the last one picked. In other areas, I overcompensated and became the overachiever, seeking the approval of those who mattered. It took the better part of my lifetime to realize that these experiences had sowed the seeds for a dark side, one that curtailed my leadership capacity.

One of the classes I took in Transformational Leadership at Bethel University involved analyzing our leadership and spiritual development, based on *The Making of a Leader: Recognizing the Lessons and Stages of Leadership Development* by Dr. Robert J. Clinton. By mapping and scrutinizing the patterns in my own life, I began to see how my countless "negative" experiences—filled with hurt, pain, frustration, and anger—were actually strengthening moments since I was forced to focus my attention in new directions. Clinton calls these tough times "negative preparation."

So, when I looked at those "negatives" in light of my leadership and spiritual development, I was able to reframe and redeem those experiences. Emotional healing happened for me as I brought those difficult times, one by one, into the light with a trusted mentor.

What experiences did you have growing up that might have developed a dark side, an extra-sensitive area, in your inner being?

Millennials and Their Emotional Dark Sides

Many of the young leaders we coach are affected by emotional scars. When they choose to ignore or hide those scars, it negatively impacts their leadership potential, which greatly inhibits their ability to positively influence others now and in the future. This should be a growth area for many of us, but I believe millennials have the most to gain if they can correct this now.

Sociologist Donna Freitas, author of *The Happiness Effect: How Social Media is Driving a Generation to Appear Perfect at Any Cost*, agrees that this new generation wrestles with unique issues. In today's world, there's a default expectation that you should manage your personal brand, always presenting yourself as happy, successful, and having your act together at all times. There's no safe place to be vulnerable.

Millennials, like everyone, experience fear and uncertainty. Where can they candidly discuss what they are really thinking and feeling? Who can they confide in about the darkness? Yes, some will say they can tell their tribe of friends, but those people tend to be so like-minded that often there isn't someone who can speak truth into their lives.

This is where a wise mentor is vital. Here are some signs that help me identify someone who is struggling:

- Overreaction: Reactions are intense and extreme and don't fit the situation. For example, sadness becomes overwhelming despair and anger quickly turns to rage.
- Underreaction: Reactions are bottled up. Their face shows little emotion. They might not respond to the topic we're discussing, or they'll change the focus of the conversation.
- Interpersonal reaction: They struggle to handle one-on-one conflict. They look to other people for support and approval, thinking it will reduce their anxiety.

Work with Your Next-Gen Leader to Deal with Their Dark Side

One of my go-to resources in this area is *Overcoming the Dark Side of Leadership: The Paradox of Personal Dysfunction* by Dr. Sam Rima and Gary L. McIntosh. When any of the following unhealthy leadership patterns or characteristics are exposed, it's a sign to dig deeper:

- Compulsiveness
- Narcissism
- Paranoia
- Codependency
- Passive-aggressiveness

Help your mentee realize their dark side need not leave them feeling ashamed. Instead, bringing the issues into the light can affect a course change toward emotional, intellectual, and spiritual well-being. Discuss the following with them.

Accept Reality

Prompt your young leader to accept reality without blaming others. They need to be honest and identify areas in their life where their past is affecting their leadership and sales ability in a negative way. Share with them a time in your life where you learned this lesson.

Play the Name Game

I often find that people struggle to express their true feelings, especially when those feelings and emotions are about their dark side. Help your leader to come up with the words for those emotions they are not naturally comfortable expressing. This can only be done in a trusting relationship, so be certain to share your related experiences also.

A WORD FROM A MILLENNIAL …

"Even though we seem glued to our screens, we need person-to-person contact. We can get a million likes but still feel empty from the lack of encouragement. We need to hear affirmations from others so that we get to know ourselves."

Shine the Light

Our memories of the past often include darkness. In our mind's eye, memories can make everything appear dark and dreary. However, as we picture the scene of each negative memory, we can change the lighting and the colors to ones that we like. That way we can change the heavy impact this experience has on us. Recoloring and reframing the memory can loosen its grip on us.

Ask Questions

One of my go-to questions, which I learned to ask from a mentor of mine, is, "Where do you see God in this, if at all?" Every time I ask, I get some kind of answer. Whatever the answer, it provides an open door to talk about God, the ultimate Healer.

Sleep Intentionally

Recent brain research, written about by Pollack and Cabane, reveals that we can actually rewire our thinking by being intentional in what we feed our brains before we go to sleep. We can heal our deep soul wounds by turning off the technology at least thirty minutes before going to sleep so that we can read positive affirmations or meditate on Scripture. According to Pollack and Cabane, "Your brain cleans itself out when you sleep—your brain cells shrinking by up to 60 percent to create space for your glial gardeners to come in take away the waste and prune the synapses."[1] So proactively discuss sleep habits with your next-gen leader.

We are humans, living with other humans. We will get wounded as we walk through life. However, those wounds, even if they came in first grade, can be catalysts for a deep, internal, abiding confidence—provided we are proactive in dealing with them and don't let them poison our root system.

LEADERSHIP LESSON

Keep vigilant watch over your heart;
that's where life starts. —PROVERBS 4:23

12

Set Goals to Fuel Energy

Never forgetting the pain of being the last one picked for kickball in first grade, I was determined to find something in which I could excel. My mom thought piano lessons would be a great way for me to learn persistence, resilience, and goal-setting.

The large inherited upright piano took up most of my parents' bedroom in our eight-hundred-square-foot house. Mom listened to me practice my scales until I learned to play them perfectly. Then I kept playing them. I must have played those scales five hundred times.

Studying piano aligned perfectly with some of my strengths. According to StrengthsFinder, a popular inventory authored by Tom Rath to help people find their natural strengths, I'm defined as a Maximizer, so I like everything to be excellent. That's why I practiced the scales over and over. Looking back, it now makes sense why my mom worked outside so much of the time while I practiced piano!

My other strength, according to the StrengthsFinder inventory, is Achiever. In order to feel good about myself, I must feel like I've accomplished something that I can cross off my to-do list by the end of the day. I loved polishing each measure and finalizing each piano piece so I could move on to the next.

Did I enjoy every minute of it? Certainly not. I often felt like giving up. But I eventually conquered many pieces, including Beethoven's complicated and fast-moving "Piano Sonata No. 8 in C minor," also known as "Sonata Pathétique." It is a creative masterpiece that continues to capture my imagination.

My mom had been right. Through my piano studies, I learned the value of setting goals.

What activities helped you learn the importance of setting goals? Was there a mentor or coach who inspired or supported you in the process?

Millennials and Goal-Setting

Millennials are the "now" generation. They've grown up in an age of instant gratification. Smartphones, tablets, instant messaging, and immediate access to a world of information is the norm.

Setting goals and steadily working toward them over a period of time seems like a foreign concept to some millennials. Their parents handicapped them by protecting them at every corner rather than encouraging self-reliance. They thought they were being good parents by doing portions of their children's homework, resolving conflicts on their behalf, and constantly telling their kids how "special" they were, whether the kids did anything extraordinary or not.

As I pointed out earlier, more and more millennials are struggling with depression. They're suffering because they don't have enough external motivators and they don't know how to generate enough internal motivation. This has the potential to severely impact their ability to set and reach healthy personal and business goals.

Show Your Next-Gen Leader How
to Set and Reach Goals

Why is personal goal-setting an important step in developing good self-care skills? Because if we don't set our own goals, chances are that someone else will. The result? We'll be living our lives according to someone else's agenda, and that's not fulfilling in the least. It's crucial that seasoned leaders model goal-setting and the slow, steady work it takes to achieve those goals.

I've been a long-time partner with Objective Management Group, a pioneer in the sales industry for sales-force evaluations and sales candidate screenings. They document that high achievers set goals 100 percent of the time, while low performers do so only 16 percent of the time. One of my favorite mentors, the late Zig Ziglar, said, "If you aim at nothing, you will hit it every time."[1]

Consider the following tips when mentoring your emerging leader on goal-setting.

Use a Goal-Alignment Process

Clarity on personal goals is important. So is focus on professional goals. However, your young leader will gain the most traction when they're confident that their life goals are integrated, supporting each other. My e-book, *Energize Your Dreams* (available at DanitaBye.com) is packed with goal-setting and goal-alignment ideas. It provides questions and structure so that your young leader can work through these three areas:

- Future: We help them determine where they want to be in life five to ten years from now, in all areas of their life (relationally, physically, intellectually, spiritually, and financially).
- Now: We help them discern where they are now in life in each of those areas. Also, we invite them to think about what energizes them and what de-energizes them.
- Action: We help them weave all these insights together to chart a daily and weekly move-forward plan.

A WORD FROM A MILLENNIAL ...

"Many of my friends set goals not only professionally but also personally. We share them with each other and speak as if they've happened. Plus, I see a growing debt-free mind-set. I've found twenty- and thirty-year-olds are setting themselves up to rely on their savings and income rather than government programs they can't trust."

Be SMART

Goal-setting is a tough process. Someone asks us to describe or set a goal, and our minds go blank. Sometimes short-term objectives are obvious, but the long-term goals are fuzzy. Other times, long-term vision is a snap but the next step seems unclear. SMART goals help your next-gen leader to convert his or her dreams, aspirations, and goals into reality. Goals must be:

- Specific
- Measurable
- Attainable
- Realistic
- Timely

Stay on Track

Work with your mentee to set aside time on a daily, weekly, and monthly basis to review and revise their goals, especially when they experience a loss of direction. Share your personal practices for keeping yourself on track.

A WORD FROM A MILLENNIAL ...

"Millennials aren't content with the way things have been done. Our entrepreneurial, sometimes defiant attitudes cause us to question. Although this can be really frustrating (for you and for us), it can lead to incredible progress and positive change. Our generation possesses the courage to challenge the status quo for the greater good. So, we love when others can help us convert the energy into action."

Shift to a Growth Mind-set

Talents, skills, and perspectives aren't set in stone. They can all grow and be strengthened with focus and effort. Brainstorm with your mentee to explore how they might leverage their struggles of today to make the situations better tomorrow. Instead of allowing them to complain or pass blame, ask how they might capitalize on a seemingly overwhelming problem, so they move closer to the goal. By adjusting their mind-set, they can find creative solutions.

Even though the classic piano is becoming antiquated in our technology-driven world, I still sit down at my baby grand piano periodically to play the Pathétique sonata. My fingers and brain synapses are a bit rusty; however, playing reminds me of the importance of helping our next-gen leaders to make goal-setting a habit, so they can enjoy the benefits of a healthy root system for a lifetime.

LEADERSHIP LESSON

Compelling, heartfelt goals give
hope and drive.

13

Establish a Rest Rhythm

I vividly remember the struggles I had with work-life balance when we were building our house and our first daughter was due to be born soon. My awareness journey to reconnect with my inner self highlighted the counter productiveness of trying to keep too many balls in the air at the same time.

When I learned to practice self-care, the first thing I discovered was the need for a new work-rest rhythm. I committed to prioritize time every day to become more aware of where I was physically, intellectually, emotionally, and spiritually. I had to work hard to understand what was happening in each of those areas. This exercise required me to be still, and that was asking a lot.

But I don't give up easily. I started training myself to meditate. Every time I became quiet, focusing became easier. During these quiet times, I received insight into the problem areas of my personal and professional life. Most importantly, I realized that in order to take care of anyone else in a healthy way, I needed to care for my internal world.

Giving ourselves permission to pause our frenzied schedules is okay. In fact, it's necessary for sustainable effective leadership. As we mentor core character traits in millennials, we need to energize them to map a well-balanced work-rest rhythm so that they can be healthy in all areas of their lives.

Millennials and the Work-Rest Tension

A 2015 survey, "Stress in America," revealed that millennials are the most stressed-out generation of all Americans.[1] We all know that stress has been linked to higher blood pressure, insomnia, and unhealthy coping behaviors, like substance abuse. Another seemingly enjoyable activity, spending too much time on social media, is now also regarded as a contributing cause of stress and depression.

A WORD FROM A MILLENNIAL ...

"We are particularly at risk here because of the inexhaustible flow of information and stimulation at our fingertips 24/7. Our access to everything risks that we focus on nothing."

According to a recent *Forbes* article, researchers at the University of Pittsburgh School of Medicine conducted a study about the effects of social media habits on the moods of users. They found that the more time young adults use social media, the more likely they are to sink into depression. Why is this? Some analyzers speculate that it's easy to create a distorted picture of a happy, successful life on social media. When these embellished existences are compared to their own, young people may feel that their lives are inferior and less successful, causing anxiety and depression.[2]

Even more disturbing is that social media consumes time that could have been used to relax, meditate, or sleep. These practices are certainly not conducive to a healthy work-rest rhythm.

How can we help millennials develop good self-care routines in this area of their lives so that they flourish?

A WORD FROM A MILLENNIAL ...

"Our biggest strength is also our biggest weakness. Our generation is more aware of the world around us. On one hand, we are more aware and conscious of the hot-topic issues that plague not only our country, but our entire world: poverty, global warming, race, abuse. Anything that scrolls across our iPhones, we know about. This makes us more informed politically, socially, and emotionally. However, our generation hasn't found this in moderation, but rather saturation. As a collective group, we spend countless hours staring at a screen. We look for the acceptance of our peers in the form of likes on a post. This self-awareness is our downfall. We may know a lot about the world around us, maybe even too much on occasion, but hardly ever do you see a young adult know as much about themselves as they do the issues they care about."

Show Your Next-Gen Leader How to Establish a Healthy Work-Rest Rhythm

No one golden rule will miraculously work for every up-and-coming leader to establish a healthy work-rest rhythm. But with your experience in business and life, you can help guide them toward a place where they devote their time and energy wisely.

Our Creator crafted each of us uniquely. Therefore, it seems reasonable that we each have a distinctive pattern in how we balance work and rest mentally, emotionally, and spiritually. Help your leader find the best way to determine the pace that allows them to proactively nurture their roots.

Schedule Reflection Time

Motivate your leader to block out a larger block of resting and reflection time on a monthly or quarterly basis. Experienced leaders I observe have a variety of resting and reflection disciplines they practice. Here are some ideas you can use to stimulate your young leader to experiment in developing their own rhythm:

- Schedule time each day to get outdoors. Take a book or a Bible, along with a notebook, to record new insights.

- Use a personal SWOT: think through the Strengths, Weaknesses, Opportunities, and Threats you are experiencing. Then use that awareness to devise an action plan.

Create the Top Ten Questions

Guide your next-gen leader to create a set of top ten questions they want to ask themselves every month. They could be leadership questions—whether professional, personal, or both. They could be questions on how they're living out their values, or questions on how they're doing relationally, physically, emotionally, spiritually, and/or financially.

Draft a Life Map

An engineering friend of mine has mapped out three sets of objectives:

- Outward: How might I act justly with mercy to the hurting world around me?
- Inward: How might I love with mercy and minister to key relationships?
- Upward: How might I walk humbly with my Creator?

He has tactics, goals, and strategies tied to each of these objectives. It's a bit analytical, but it works for him as a great reflection tool to ensure each area of his life is on purpose.

Recognize Your Spiritual Pathway

In the appendix of my book *Letters from the King: A Devotional Parable of Spiritual Discovery*, I included a survey that readers can use to help them figure out some of the ways, based on their unique wiring, that they can strengthen themselves mentally, emotionally, and spiritually. I've added it to the appendix of this book as well (see page 229). As you work through the survey with your mentee, you may even discover some new spiritual pathways for yourself.

A Day of Rest

The Hebrew word *Sabbath* means a day of rest. Regardless of whether or not you hold to a set of spiritual beliefs, most people agree that a period of rest is essential to regain and maintain physical strength and mental well-being.

Assist your emerging leader to draw up a list of ideas to make the most of their day. Here are a few ideas:

- Declare a tech downtime for a certain part of the day.
- Commit to visiting someone you haven't seen in the last month.
- Take a walk in a park or a nature reserve.

Benjamin Franklin said, "He that can take rest is greater than he that can take cities." A healthy work-rest rhythm is not a luxury but a necessity. Trying to keep too many balls in the air will eventually result in a ball falling to the ground. And we know what happens next—they usually all bite the dust. Help millennials to plan, prioritize, and practice keeping a healthy work-rest rhythm so that they regain their physical, intellectual, emotional, and spiritual well-being. It's good for the roots.

LEADERSHIP LESSON

A healthy work-rest rhythm helps us regain
and maintain physical, intellectual,
emotional, and spiritual strength.

Dear Reader,

Discernment and wisdom are often born in the crucible of life. We have experienced and fought our way back from fatigue, loss of passion, burnout, and even moral and ethical failures. We know the importance of taking care of our inner world, and of taking care of our root system.

Your depth and breadth of insights can inspire your next-gen leader to develop a deep, robust root system that will sustain them, their families, and their followers for the long haul. May your leadership legacy be born in those who are stable enough to withstand the tornado-force winds of this culture and strong enough to positively influence the trajectory of your business and our culture.

> *Happy are those who reject the advice of evil people, who do not follow the example of sinners or join those who have no use for God. Instead, they find joy in obeying the Law of the* LORD, *and they study it day and night. They are like trees that grow beside a stream, that bear fruit at the right time, and whose leaves do not dry up. They succeed in everything they do.*
> PSALM 1:1–3 GNT

—Danita

Interview with Jeff Pelletier of Life's Core Purpose

Dantotsu. Have you heard this word before? It's a Japaneese word that means "best of the best." The concept of benchmarking is based on this principle. It is easy to see how best-of-the-best thinking applies to manufacturing and production. But, how can it be applied to sales, sales management, and leadership on a consistent basis?

Jeff Pelletier has answered that question. He advocates that we are at our best when we are living and working at the intersection of two core concepts. First, that we operate within our natural gifts and strengths, which we do without even thinking. Second, that we focus on that which we care passionately about.

I have family, friends, clients, and colleagues who are re-energized after working through Jeff's proven process.

Q: Jeff, tell us about yourself and your vision at Life's Core Purpose.

Jeff: My vision with Life's Core Purpose is to help business owners and leaders to recruit and develop people with complementary Core Competence and Core Passion. This integration, properly led, can create businesses that maximize individual and corporate potential. Innovation, improvement, and great cultures are all possible for your business when Life's Core Purpose is managed well.

Q: That's a compelling vision. How did Life's Core Purpose come to you?

Jeff: It began with a hypothesis. Is there something I am personally great at all the time at a core level? And, is there something I care deeply about all the time at a core level? I wrestled with this hypothesis for quite some time. I finally came to the conclusion that yes, there is. And when I applied what I did well to what I cared deeply about, my performance in life and work grew exponentially.

Q: Once you made that discovery, what happened next?

Jeff: I expanded to, "If this is true of me, is it true of someone else?" So during dog walks and conversational time with my wife, Barbara, I began the process of trying to determine if these two questions could be answered in her life as well. After many hours and days, we both agreed that there was indeed something Barbara did really well all the time and something she really cared about all the time. We called what she did well her Core Competence, and we called what she cared about all the time her Core Passion.

Our next question was whether or not this is true for everyone. Though an extensive journey, we've determined that yes, it is true for everyone. It now takes an inquiring mind sixty to ninety minutes of guided self-discovery online.

Q: It's been a long, fruitful journey, Jeff. Let's apply this to what the business owners, CEOs, and presidents are telling you about their work with millennials.

Jeff: First, let me state that I have nothing but admiration for this generation, and I think America's best years are ahead of us. I'm working very hard to help as many of them as I can.

One of the characteristics of millennials that really intrigues me is that they really want their lives to be relevant and meaningful. What's wrong with that? A lot of baby boomers just want people to get the job done. Millennials are asking, "Why? What's the point? What's the purpose? Why is it important? How does it help?" I suggest that the answers to these questions can cause work to be efficient, effective, and lean. When you answer those questions, work can be more productive. Since most successful business owners are "bottom line" people, this should be a win-win.

Q: What do you see going wrong in business climates today?

Jeff: If I have an employee and I just want them to show up and do their job (provide them with skills to advance the work and create more business), and these employees are millennials, I can expect this group to have pretty high turnover. And if I treat that millennial with a mild impatience that usually accompanies a predetermined opinion, I can expect to accelerate that turnover. This is a lose-lose outcome.

Q: Sometimes business leaders think this high turnover is due to lack of resiliency. In your experience, what's the connection between resiliency and our Life's Core Purpose?

Jeff: There's a deep connection. When a person understands their Life's Core Purpose and they trip, fall, or hit obstacles on either a personal or professional front, they can get back into the game more quickly.

If I know these two things about myself, (1) what I'm great at and (2) what I care deeply about, then I know exactly how to use that to get back in the game. This causes resilience. It gives me a life's focus that transcends my job or any circumstance.

Q: So would it be helpful for a manager to know someone's Life Core Purpose so that they might better encourage their next-gen leader?

Jeff: I recently worked with a millennial who owns a commercial real estate business, as he went through the Life's Core Purpose process. Once he had his purpose defined, we began to talk about how valuable it would be to have his group understand each other's Life Core Purpose. In understanding one another on this level, they could learn how to support and complement one another. It could be a powerful competitive advantage for his team. He scheduled a team workshop.

Q: What were some of the outcomes of this workshop?

Jeff: It was amazing! Right away, he started making decisions and correcting himself for how he was utilizing their talent. Plus, he moved people to different positions in the company because he realized where they would be happier and more productive.

Q: So, as each person has a deeper understanding of their Life's Core Purpose and are willing to share that with people on their team, they are more aligned and more engaged. I would imagine higher work output, more productivity, and higher retention?

Jeff: Yes. The other thing it does is it helps employees better self-manage. If they're in a job where they're great at what they do and they care about what they accomplish, less supervision is needed. This allows management to do strategic work and think more about the future.

Q: Most of us love the self-managing concept.

Jeff: I've come to see that your core competence empowers your StrengthsFinder results. Your strengths empower your passion. They work together.

Q: If you were to give business owners and leaders a couple of key insights as they are coaching, mentoring, and leading the millennials in their life, what would be some core recommendations?

Jeff: First, do not underestimate them. That will be the biggest mistake you can make. Next, challenge them appropriately. A challenge is something I can do, but I have to stretch. It is not an overwhelming thing, but I need to stretch in order to accomplish it. If every business owner did these two things with millennials, they would be really impressed with the results.

Q: Great insights, Jeff. Any other closing words of wisdom for leaders in working with their next-gen leader?

Jeff: To me there are two key outcomes when it comes to managing and leading millennials. Be real. As a rule, they *hate* pretense and hypocrisy. They love authenticity. And since they are seeking to fulfill their potential in life, provide opportunity, encourage innovation, and provide positive accountability.

Q: I heard you have a discount code for our readers. Tell us about that.

Jeff: Our research indicates that by the sheer number of millennials going through it, that finding and living Life's

Core Purpose has a very high value to this group. It's easy and inexpensive to sponsor someone in this personal discovery. Simply have them go tolifescorepurpose. com and click on *Find Yours*. At checkout, they enter the promotional code DANITA17 and will receive half off the regular price. This gives them access to the discovery video where they can download the accompanying worksheet. They also will receive our regular Purpose Tips via e-mail and have access to other tools to help them live out their Life's Core Purpose.

Section 2

Lead with Confidence

Kind words can be short
and easy to speak, but their
echoes are truly endless.

—Mother Teresa

Part 1

Model an Impact Mind-set

Definition: A high appreciation for your work that is aligned with your unique wiring and calling so that one is a confident contributor.

The Impact Mind-set and Leadership

The voice on the other end of the phone call sounded confused and frustrated. The young salesperson, Sarah, was a few months into her new job. She'd hit a rocky road in her current position and needed a career-coaching session.

During the session, she told me in confidence, "It feels as if all my dreams and goals that my boss and I discussed during my interview have disappeared. When I try to talk to him about other ideas on how to reach the goal, he just tells me to focus on what he wants me to do, and that's it. I'm supposed to just focus on 'hitting the number.' He's not listening to me. It feels like he only cares about his agenda, not mine. I really think I should look for another job where I can be myself, be an integral part of the team versus just a number, and be a leader."

A WORD FROM A MILLENNIAL ...

"This would be an incredible irritant to a millennial, because many pride themselves on creativity, problem-solving, and considering new perspectives."

Putting on my sales-coach hat, I asked Sarah to think through at least three possible reasons the boss might be responding this way, and at least three possible solutions, then we could discuss deeper and develop a win-win action plan. We also discussed what she appreciated about her work, and how aligned her job was with her interests, talents, and passions.

This turned out to be a great leadership growth opportunity for Sarah. However, this isn't an isolated case. Young leaders say they're invigorated and motivated when they feel they're making an impact. When they're not, they are more prone to become disengaged and bored with their work. When this happens, a loss of productivity is guaranteed.

Who's been a supportive confidant for you as you've pondered the purpose and meaning of your work?

Appreciation and Alignment Leadership Framework

Leaders whose work is aligned with their talents and strengths, and who have a high appreciation for their work, are filled with purpose. This alignment of strengths and appreciation while working gives them an impact mind-set. These leaders are engaged and valuable contributors at work, seeing alignment between their personal and professional goals. This creates synergy on both home and work fronts. Such leaders are confident yet humble contributors of ideas and solutions, shedding light on most any situation, like lighthouses to those around them.

Other leaders are frustrated. This stems from utilizing their gifts and talents at work but not in intentional or focused ways.

It's hard for them to see their contributions to their work teams. Since these leaders aren't intentionally focusing their passions, their impact potential is curtailed.

An inability to connect what they're doing today with what they want to be doing in the future is disheartening for both them and you. With an internal light that is dimming, they are increasingly discouraged. Many frustrated leaders are probably looking to make a job move but don't know where or what they're really searching for.

On the other hand, I often see a group of twenty-something leaders who want to have meaning and purpose at work, but they also know there's a misalignment with their gifts and talents. This is also a frustrating and confusing stage of career development. They could be A players in the company, but they aren't operating in the sweet spot of their gifting, so they become C players. They often feel like they're on a treadmill, working but not getting anywhere. Confidence is shaken for this group of young leaders. As you're coaching and mentoring millennials, you might also encounter the "my job has no meaning or purpose" frustration. What other frustrations and job/talent alignment issues do you see among your millennials? We can use our experience to model an impact mind-set as we help mentees gain clarity on how they can align their gifts and talents with the work they do.

Millennials and the Impact Mind-set

Only 12 percent of those participating in our "Millennial Matters" survey said that one of the biggest concerns was their young leader's disregard for the value of work. Yet a recent Gallup study on millennials found that employees twenty to thirty-six years old are the least engaged generation in the workplace, by far.[1] This is a concern for business leaders committed to growing their companies and reducing employee turnover.

All the research on employee engagement suggests that those companies with the highest employee engagement reap the following rewards:

- 10 percent better customer ratings
- 17 percent more productive
- 21 percent more profitable
- 41 percent less absenteeism

So why are many millennials unhappy in their jobs? A video episode of *Inside Quest* called "Millennials in the Workplace," by millennial expert Simon Sinek, went viral on YouTube. In the video, Sinek states that millennials live less compartmentalized lives than their parents did. By contrast, they seek a more integrated work-life situation that enables them to meet new people, make friends, and learn new skills. Sinek also explains that it is vital to many millennials that their work and life be connected to a larger purpose.

About 60 percent of millennials say they're floating their resumes right now.[2] Guiding millennials so they figure out how to catch a sense of purpose creates a win-win culture. When employees are engaged, they're more likely to succeed and even overachieve. And when we invest in the next generation of leaders, our businesses grow and we leave a positive leadership fingerprint on those we mentor.

A WORD FROM A MILLENNIAL ...

"Can it be sufficient that millennials experience purpose? I would say that millennials can sniff out disingenuous motives in a heartbeat. We know when the only goal is bottom-line profitability."

So, what can leaders do?

Encourage Millennials to Grapple with Limitations on Purpose

I learned about an ancient Hebrew word in my Transformational Leadership studies; this word was used for both work and worship: *avodah*. Having one word for such different meanings really caused me to think. Historically, our Western culture has divided life into secular and sacred. Work is secular. Purpose and meaning are spiritual.

We, both baby boomers and millennials, wrestle with purpose. Retiring baby boomers are having purpose crises as they plan their next life stages, while millennials want purposeful lives but don't know how to bring that about. They feel left in the dark.

We struggle with how our everyday work has meaning and purpose. Most of us spend over half of our time at work. Some of us love our work, while others feel trapped and disengaged. In either case, it can be easy to disconnect our faith from our work. We often think about how work makes us feel, versus looking at the bigger, broader, and brighter purpose for being at work.

A number of years ago, I began to ask myself what might happen if I saw my work with a spiritual significance, an *avodah* perspective. Where were the daily practical opportunities to serve God through serving my colleagues and clients?

The YouTube video "Work as Worship" by RightNow Media[3] is a great summary of the struggle between what is work and what has spiritual meaning. Where is the dividing line? Or, is there one? This resource helps millennials as they seek out the purpose of their own lives and how they can be a light in their current work environment.

When we reorient our thinking, our work can be sacred, no matter what our job title. Our purpose can be woven into our work life. God's original design for us is that we would have an uninterrupted way of living, finding long-term purpose and meaning in all of life, even our work life. We are reminded that God is a worker. He started out creating. In fact, one of the first things he created was light. And, being made in his image, we don't stop flourishing just because we are working. On the contrary, that's how we flourish.

Experienced business leaders have the opportunity to teach next-gen leaders that how they do their "ordinary" work becomes "extraordinary" when they see it as a way to honor God and to serve their clients and colleagues.

For some, this will mean working to solve social issues on a big stage. For others, it'll mean making a positive impact on a colleague or client. Even if someone doesn't have a strong personal faith, they can find purpose beyond themselves within the context of their work.

For high-character value-driven leaders, this is an area where we can proactively and positively influence emerging leaders. By sharing the successes, failures, and longings to live life with purpose and meaning, we can fuel healthy professional and personal growth. Even as we need mentees to gain a deeper understanding of how their world is shifting and changing, they need our wisdom, as experienced leaders, in order to hit sustainable leadership home runs.

As I reflect on recent coaching conversations, I stand amazed at the trajectory of my own life's work. My three passions—sales leadership, millennial mentoring, and character development—are intersecting. I'm working in my sweet spot, despite the fact that I pursued a career I thought was not aligned with my dream.

How can you persuade your future leader to develop a high appreciation for their work that is aligned with their unique wiring and calling, so that they are a confident contributor and let their light shine?

A WORD FROM A MILLENNIAL …

"As much as the millennials are eager to give back and help others, we are all different in our own way. Getting to know each person and how they work is the strongest tool a leader can have."

LEADERSHIP LESSON

When you live and lead with a sacred perspective, you develop the empowered ability to become a positive agent of change.

15

Live with a High
Regard for Your Work

In my early twenties, before I was hired on at Xerox, I thought I had it all mapped out. My life dream was crystal clear. I would graduate from the university, work to save enough money for medical school, and then journey to Africa to serve as a doctor and medical missionary. I completed the first part of my plan by graduating from the university. Next up, employment. But I walked out of the first nine interviews despondent. I felt like a misfit, thinking there was no job on earth for me where I could make a real impact until I could become a doctor.

My best offer was from Frank, the hiring officer for Xerox. *Xerox?* I'd never heard of them. I'd been raised in a homestead shack without running water, let alone a copier. Plus, I was a premed major who lived in the genetics lab.

Naive and still holding onto my dream, I told Frank, "Thanks, but no thanks. A sales career is not part of my dream."

But Frank saw something in me that he wanted on the sales team, so he kept pursuing. And Frank was determined. Despite our previous meetings, which were followed by my previous nos, he asked me to a final meeting in his office on the seventh floor of the NW Bank building in downtown Sioux Falls. I ended the interview with, "Frank, I've run out of ways to say no. I'm not coming to work with you." I walked out of his office, convinced that my calling was to be a medical missionary.

However, God had other plans for me.

I walked into an empty elevator and pressed G. I needed to get to the ground floor and move on with my life the way I had it mapped out. As the doors closed, I sensed a voice that reached to the core of my being. I turned around. The elevator was still empty. After a few moments of confusion, I recognized the voice as God. He lovingly and kindly said, "Danita, I need you to say yes."

I instantly replied, "No! I already have a plan for my life. I'm going to be a medical missionary in Africa."

Have you ever done that? Reply with a defiant no, like a two-year-old, because you're certain it's the right thing to do?

The voice persisted, "Say yes, Danita. I'm calling you to be a minister in the business world, to be my ambassador, and to serve all those you meet."

You've got to be kidding me! Give up my African dream for this?

We've all had a similar choice, haven't we? You probably didn't receive your wake-up call in an empty elevator, but you know there's a call on your life, a call to make a difference. You have a desire to serve, to leave a leadership legacy that extends beyond yourself.

So what did I do with the message all those years ago? I telephoned Frank, the hiring officer at Xerox, and said, "Hi, Frank, this is Danita. I guess I'm coming to work with you after all."

And I started my career in North Dakota, not Africa. Sales, not medical missions. Frank was my new boss. And soon the new possibilities lit me up.

What was your dream job? How were you going to change the world?

Millennials and the Glamour-Job Myth

According to a Gallup survey published in *Business Journal*, 71 percent of millennials who strongly agree that they know what their company stands for and how they're different from their competitors, indicate they plan to stay employed with their current company for at least the next year.[1]

Meaning and purpose are paramount for up-and-coming leaders. Many struggle to see the impact of their jobs, sharing thoughts like the following:

- "My sales work isn't important enough to make a meaningful difference."
- "My work isn't happening on a big-enough stage to have a lasting impact."
- "My work has nothing to do with my real passions of helping the world."

As a rule, millennials want to understand how their jobs fit with the big picture. They want to know that the boss sees them as a vital component to carrying out the larger vision of the company. They want to see a certain glamour in what they do.

When the grand vision is shared with them, they gain a sense of purpose, which makes them feel like an important part of the team. Casting vision and confirming company values are must-haves in a business owner's attraction and retention strategy, particularly if they're building their business growth and transition strategies on integrating millennials into their team.

Bust the Glamour-Job Myth
for Your Next-Gen Leader

What about your next-gen leader? What's the connection between their "glamour" job and what they're doing today? Ask them if they see the connection between their long-term vision and the work they're doing now.

No matter how glamorous or unglamorous their job might feel to them, you can inspire them to discover that all of life, including work life, has a spiritual, high-impact dimension. It's a myth that a "bigger purpose" means "feeding the whole world … today." "High impact" means to be intentional and purposeful about even the smallest of intentions and interactions.

Here are some ideas for how to mentor having a high regard for one's work.

Align Vision and Values

Ask your young leader, especially if they're unhappy in their current job, if they know the company vision and values. If yes, ask them questions like these:

- What do you think about the company's vision and values?
- What alignment do you see between the company's vision and values and your own?
- What synergy, if any, do you see?
- How do you see yourself fitting into the big picture?

These questions are important to grapple with in any season of life, including as a young leader.

Address the What, the How, and the Way

It's easy for all of us to get caught up in thinking that what we achieve is most important, or that how we look and the image we project while we're achieving is. As seasoned leaders, we know that success starts with our core character. It's the way we do our work that is memorable and impactful, especially honoring and serving others respectfully. Talk through this statement with your next-gen leader and get their insights: *It's not what I do, or how I look, but the way I do my work that ignites my ability to be a positive change agent.*

Speak "I Choose ..." Affirmations

Words, spoken internally to ourselves and externally to the world, are powerful. Does your mentee know the power of their words?

Dr. Caroline Leaf, in *Switch on Your Brain: The Key to Peak Happiness, Thinking, and Health*, states that the way our brains work, our neuroplasticity, can work for us or against us. How? "Because whatever we think about the most *will grow*—this applies to both the positive and negative ends of the spectrum."[2]

Science is proving that our brains are designed to grow that which we think about most. Does your leader know this about their brain?

When we shift our work to see it as important, everything changes. Guide your mentee to edit and personalize "I choose..." affirmations such as these:

- "I choose to view the work I do now as important."
- "I choose to be intentional about the position I hold right now."
- "I choose to start making a difference today and not to bide my time until the perfect job comes along."

A WORD FROM A MILLENNIAL ...

"I want to know the reason I am saying or doing something. I want to talk about that with my mentor, if possible. I also want to hear my mentor talk about her journey of discovering the deep significance and purpose she gets from her work."

When I first turned down Frank's offer for a sales job, I'd had no idea how my life would turn out. It's both humbling and fascinating to look back and see how everything has been creatively woven together. When we live with a high regard for our work, we begin to discover many places where we can shine our light in whatever work environment we find ourselves. Even a sales and leadership work life can provide an opportunity for high-impact service.

A WORD FROM A MILLENNIAL …

"Mentors can provide a 'thirty-thousand-foot view' for millennials and help us see the impact that we might not see. Help millennials see that their impact has a domino effect that can shift relationships, structures, and even professions."

LEADERSHIP LESSON

Find purpose in what you do and
take pride in your work.

Prioritize Now to Impact the Future

"I'm wasting precious time in this job."

My friend Chuck was questioning the value of his role as a human resource leader in a large company with a growing African immigrant employee base. He'd written his resignation letter and was ready to submit it. Over coffee, he confessed, "I'm wasting time here. I should be where the African people really need my help." He was seriously considering leaving his family here in the United States and dedicating the rest of his life to work in Tanzania, Africa, where he could do what he believed was important.

Chuck hadn't fully embraced his present situation, making him blind to the opportunity for impact that was before him. Essentially, Africa had come to him, and he was already doing important work!

This is a truth for many of us. We often fail to see the opportunities in our present situation, even opportunities for ways to affirm millennials who are square in our pathways.

Millennials and the Now-or-Never Myth

Many millennials ask, "How does my 'ordinary work' fit into my dream of being a person of impact, my dream of making a real difference in the world?"

The "Deloitte Millennial Survey for 2016" reports that when organizations show they have a purpose that goes deeper than increased revenues, it increases loyalty. Also, the stats on those intending to stay for longer than five years goes up significantly.[1]

What does this tell us about millennials? They want to feel that what they are doing now matters.

Impatience often prevents millennials from focusing on the potential importance of their present situation. This need for instant gratification, which is a common expectation in our modern, microwave culture, sets them up to fall for the now-or-never myth.

I call them the "snap generation." It seems they expect to snap their fingers and get everything on their bucket list accomplished within short order. There's a fear that if it doesn't happen now, it never will.

Yet, the truth is that "now" is tightly connected to "then." It's a series of snaps, not a single snap. What they do now (today) has a dramatic long-term impact on their skills, strengths, and capacities of then (tomorrow).

Shatter the Now-or-Never Myth for Your Next-Gen Leader

In retrospect, if I'd worked more closely with my mentors and coaches, I might have reframed my sales career at Xerox and arrived at a different conclusion. For example, I might have seen value in encouraging each person I interacted with in the sales process. Or I could have found fulfillment in knowing that I was helping the business run more effectively and efficiently, creating more high-paying, stable jobs in the community.

A WORD FROM A MILLENNIAL ...

"I've heard we are known as the 'me' generation, but I see one of our biggest strengths as our willingness to help others and be there when someone is in a time of need. We care passionately for others."

How might you embolden your young leader to recognize that the work they are doing today lays the foundation for tomorrow? This cognition is critical if they are to develop their full capacity as a sales and entrepreneurial leader in the long haul. However, it might be hard for them to see beyond the perceived shadows and drudgery of their daily tasks and monthly goals. Here are some ideas to facilitate the topic for discussion.

Adopt the Common-Denominator Philosophy

This inspiring quote is as applicable today as it was in 1940 when it was first delivered by Albert E. N. Gray: "The common denominator of success—the secret of success for every person who has ever been successful—lies in the fact that they formed the habit of doing things that failures don't like to do."[2] Share that quote with your mentee, then ask them questions like these:

- How might this concept apply to your life right now?
- What practices are you forming to help you move toward your dreams?
- What habits might be derailing you and holding you back?

As you talk with your next-gen leader, talk about the anatomy of a habit: a behavior or action, a cue that signals when you are to do the action, and a reward to celebrate the accomplishment of the action.[3] Also, remember to openly discuss your own habits and what's working, as well as what's not.

Counter the Imposter Syndrome

At all stages of leadership development, many of us are plagued by the imposter syndrome. That is, we feel like we're frauds. We're petrified of being exposed and everyone finding that we're fake. Following are affirmations I review when I'm filled with doubt. Discuss these, or your own affirmations, with your up-and-coming leader. If they struggle with insecurities, support them as they write their own affirmations.

- "I believe the greatest place of impact is where I am right now. My short-term focus will yield long-term results."
- "I believe I'm strategically designed to serve a specific group of people in a particular place and time to accomplish a distinct purpose."
- "I believe I have what it takes to accomplish all the purposes and plans laid out for me. This includes my relational, physical, intellectual, spiritual, and financial abilities."

A WORD FROM A MILLENNIAL …

"Keep in mind that millennials will always be millennials. Generationally speaking, we will not eventually mature into a different generation. So even though millennials are young now, we will age and mature, but the characteristics unique to the generation will remain. Give advice that will serve us well when we are seasoned business men and women."

Focus on One Step at a Time

Ask questions of your mentee so they get clarity on their futures. The clearer the picture for them, the more engaging it will be. Then work with them to convert the long-term vision into bite-sized goals, so that it's a step-by-step process. Also, talk about your long-term vision and how you've developed SMART goals for yourself.

A WORD FROM A MILLENNIAL ...

"We want to make an impact, but we have to realize that there is more to making an impact than just random action. Sometimes it takes strategy and skills."

Celebrate Small Steps

Assist your young leader in reflecting regularly (daily/weekly/monthly) on the skills they're strengthening and the knowledge they're gaining in their current work. These are paving the way toward their desired future. Celebrate their new insights. Then talk through the next steps they can take. This process gives them the opportunity to report their progress to you so that you can encourage them, spur them even further, and collaborate on more potential next steps. Plus, during this process, you'll be amazed at how much you learn as well.

Use your platform today to teach your emerging leader the true and deeper meaning of work, that they can bring light to wherever they are. Shatter their now-or-never myth. As they begin to unearth the importance and gravitas of what they're doing right now, with the people and projects they're working with and on right now, their light begins to shine. They'll be less inclined to think, like my friend did, that they have to resign themselves to a distant, far-away place. *Avodah*, where the purpose of their life is woven into their work life, starts right here.

LEADERSHIP LESSON

What we do today will have
a long-term impact for all.

17

Know
What Jazzes You

During a group meeting with young entrepreneurs, we discussed how to leverage our strengths to grow our businesses and exceed our growth goals. Suddenly one young man's eyes lit up, and he asked, "Wouldn't it be great if every moment of our workday was filled with stuff we love to do, where we're super jazzed, always operating in our sweet spot? We'd all have 100 percent job satisfaction. We could claim ultra-productive, never-stressful days. I want to be that way. How can I be jazzed 24/7?"

We all laughed and nodded in agreement even though we all knew he was describing the myth of the perfect job. However, many of us know exactly what it feels like to be jazzed, to be in the zone, to operate in our sweet spot. We've had that experience where we said, "I was born to do this!" It felt almost surreal. It was as if time came to a standstill and we could stay there forever. These moments can help focus our attention so that we're doing the work that's right for us.

When future leaders have identified tasks and priorities that keep them engrossed in their work, or when they learn to order their tasks so they're doing them in an order that fits their energy level, then they'll find a way to stay enlivened the whole day. They probably won't have the "I'm born to do this" response every day, but they're on track to doing that which is rewarding to them.

By coaching them to pay attention to what jazzes them, we invite them to live with a high regard for their work. When they stay in that place of high energy all day, becoming impactful leaders will be a natural outpouring of their souls. Remember, this generation longs to make a difference. They can't do that if they're de-energized all day long.

A WORD FROM A MILLENNIAL …

"I think people eventually become passionate about things they are good at or things they are appreciated for. Given, that could be a cause and affect thing. But I think that if someone actually focuses on being good at … rental property management … then that will lead to being passionate about it. The problem is when you never become a true student of your field where you try to be the best. That middle ground of complacency leaves you unsatisfied. I do know where this fits in, just a thought."

Millennials and the Perfect-Job Myth

Millennials have strong views about what's important to them in the workplace. Many younger sales, entrepreneurial, and business leaders believe their workday should be filled only with what they love to do, what's exciting for them to do, or what's saving the world. If it's not, they quit and find something more exciting.

As a reminder, here is what emerging leaders tell me is important about their work:

- A boss who cares about them as an individual, not just a number or a trend
- Clear expectations about what their job responsibilities are and how they'll get feedback

A WORD FROM A MILLENNIAL …

"This is huge! The most complaints I get from my friends about their boss is the fact that no one tells them something is wrong until it's too late. They want some form of constructive feedback as guidance to grow and get better at what they are doing."

This list is different from what most experienced leaders had on their lists when they were in their twenties, so it can be frustrating for many. Although, secretly, many of us admire the high ideals held by millennials. However, there are some broader cultural shifts happening that impact all of us. Millennials want:

- Regular, timely, and positive feedback on how they're doing and where they need to stretch and grow
- Intentional career development that is tied to their vision of success, so they grow in their capacities and develop skills for their future
- A company culture that values them as an entire human being, allowing them to blend work life with personal life
- Communication about how their work makes a difference in the company
- Commitment to giving back to the community and helping others

Since the financial crash, a cultural transformation has been occurring in the sales world. Historically, baby boomers have been more extrinsically motivated, such as by the size of the commission check, a high-end car, a new boat, an exotic vacation, or a cabin on the exclusive lake. However, with their bank accounts shaken by the crash, they began changing to be more intrinsically motivated, just like the millennials. Up-and-coming leaders, as well as our baby boomers, are more motivated by what they love doing, such as striving for mastery, changing the world, and doing their job for self-satisfaction.[1]

What Energizes Your Next-Gen Leader?

Every job involves elements that can either energize or de-energize us. And there are times when we're motivated by the project we're working on, and times when we aren't. But how can we motivate our rising-star leaders to become more aware of their strengths so they operate more fully in them?

No job presents the perfect set of tasks to perfectly match our skills, as we all know. However, as Tom Rath, author of *StrengthsFinder 2.0*, concludes, "When we're able to put most of our energy into developing our natural talents, extraordinary room for growth exists."[2]

So, how might you walk alongside your next-gen leader?

Keep an Energize/De-energize Journal

Suggest to your next-gen leader that they set aside time at the end of each day to reflect on what they did during the day that left them energized, jazzed. Questions to stimulate reflection might include these:

- What did I do today that felt naturally productive?
- What challenged me in a way that felt rewarding and fulfilling?
- When did I feel refreshed?
- When did I feel like I was "in the zone" and time went quickly?

Most people can identify these easily. Also ask them to think about what they did that seemed to suck the life out of them, activities that were de-energizing.

After two weeks, invite your mentee to review their journal

to see emerging trends. It's often a revelation for them to see the same energizers and de-energizers pop up day after day. Guide them to work with, or around, the de-energizers that dim their inner light.

A WORD FROM A MILLENNIAL ...

"I had a professor who told us to categorize activities as red, yellow, or green. Red: Not good at it, don't like it. Yellow: Good at it, but don't like it. Or, bad at it, but like it. Green: Good at it, and like it. He encouraged us to seek out more opportunities to work in green areas, as we would succeed and enjoy. Win-win!"

Get Insight on Natural Talents

There are numerous assessments and surveys that provide targeted insights so people get a better grasp on what their natural gifts and talents might be. This information can be helpful in identifying whether or not their current job and role are a good fit for them.

I often find that when we're focused on doing something that's a weakness, it can be particularly draining. Most leaders are high achievers and commit to anything they tackle with excellence. That's admirable. However, if we expend too much energy trying to excel in our areas of weakness, we'll eventually burn out.

Brainstorm Protection Strategies

After your up-and-coming leader identifies the tasks that deplete their energy and enthusiasm, work with them to develop strategies to deal with that task rather than avoid it altogether.

For example, I'm naturally a visionary extrovert who's jazzed when working with any leadership or sales leader who's strategic or visionary by nature. Thus, many tasks in running my sales force development and leadership development practice don't come naturally to me! I've had to develop strategies to accomplish the tasks that de-energize me. These strategies will vary with each person depending on their situation. Here are some examples:

- Outsource the task to someone who's stronger in that area.
- Reward yourself by scheduling a fun, energizing project immediately after you complete the de-energizing task.
- Ask someone to help you so that you work on it as a team.
- Break the project into bite-size pieces, tackling one part at a time.
- Set aside a certain amount of time to work on the project for today. When the buzzer rings and the time is up, celebrate what you did accomplish and create an action plan to accomplish the next step of the project.

Spur your next-gen leader to find alternative success strategies to protect themselves. This is a gift you can give them which they will be thankful for their entire life.

The perfect-job myth derails the hopes and dreams of many young leaders. We have an opportunity to influence them to realize that there is no perfect job where we are jazzed 24/7. However, those tasks where they're energized and feel like they have purpose and meaning are important. As we pay attention to what jazzes us and have a high regard for the work we're doing right now, we'll all gain clues to where we can best serve others and fuel those aspects of us to shine.

LEADERSHIP LESSON

For greater impact and influence,
learn what jazzes you.

Dear Reader,

The Purpose Driven Life, a book written by Rick Warren, has sold over 40 million copies. That's astounding.

We're in the midst of a purpose crisis. For many of us, the crisis is finding a new purpose as we enter this next stage where we'll no longer be able to define ourselves by the titles on our business cards or the companies we own. Millennials want to see their purpose now. They don't want to waste their lives. Many experienced leaders secretly envy the up-and-coming generation for being so passionate about making their lives count.

That is why I love the YouTube video "Work as Worship" by RightNow Media. If you haven't watched it yet, please do. You'll find it to be a great resource for both you and your next-gen leader as you advise each other to live confidently, with a high regard for your work, while leaning into your experiences, strengths, skills, and passions—and sharing your God-given light and brilliance with others.

> *Whatever you do, work at it with all your heart, as working for the Lord, not for human masters, since you know that you will receive an inheritance from the Lord as a reward. It is the Lord Christ you are serving.*
> COLOSSIANS 3:23–24 NIV

—Danita

Interview with Phyllis Hennecy Hendry, President/CEO of Lead Like Jesus

Some friends said, "You'll never be the same after meeting Phyllis!" They were 100 percent on target. Phyllis has a heart and passion for leaders around the world, especially the up-and-coming leaders who are our future. We have a kindred spirit.

Q: What's the vision for Lead Like Jesus and the Igniting Influence initiative with millennials?

Phyllis: Lead Like Jesus is focused on developing leaders who will lead as Jesus led. We heard that leaders were challenged by younger people in their workforce and began to think about how difficult it is to change as we get older—that we needed to train leaders to lead like Jesus sooner. We became convicted about the millennial generation and knowing that these young men and women have such a passion for character and integrity. They have a great desire to use their influence positively.

Q: How does Igniting Influence support their desire for influence?

Phyllis: Millennials often have questions about their own identity. Who are they? What is their purpose? What does that look like? What about self-worth? What about pride or fear? What about building strong relationships? In Igniting Influence, we talk about their identity in Jesus.

Q: You mentioned that they have a passion for character. When I remark about the importance of character development to some business leaders, they respond with, "You can't talk about character—that's insulting to talk with people about character. That's private." Share with us what you're seeing when discussing character formation with millennials.

Phyllis: Character is very important to millennials. They see broken families, corrupt governments, impoverished nations, and acts of terror. These are just the symptoms of a much deeper issue. They know that our world is in desperate need of good leaders.

They want to see that people are who they say they are, that people are doing great work. They want to join companies who have a greater purpose and aren't just about making money. They don't mind doing both, but they'd rather do things that have great purpose, in addition to making money. Many of the failures in business have come from doing something wrong. This behavior emanates from a character failure or a flaw from the leader. Millennials know that. They want to be a part of something different. If business leaders want to have good results and consistency in their business, they must talk about the character of their leaders.

Q: On your website, you say, "Up-and-coming leaders absolutely must know one thing: Character and integrity will eventually make or break any leader."

Phyllis: Yes, millennials need to know that they're part of a team where their leader is a person they can trust to do what he or she says. It's when words and actions match that trust is formed.

Q: We're seeing this in our work also. How do you present Jesus as their model when many millennials are un-churched or are identifying as having no religious affiliation?

Phyllis: First, Jesus, the greatest leader of all time, used his influence in the lives of twelve ordinary men to change the course of history. How would our homes, workplaces, communities, and the world look different if we allowed him to actively lead in and through us? Second, most millennials have a sense that there is a greater power or a God. Millennials don't believe life is all about them. So, we talk about who is the one that you trust the most in your life, the one that has the ultimate authority in your life even with young people that might not have a personal faith.

Q: How do you see them responding to this message?

Phyllis: Millennials have a great sense of cause and purpose around their lives. Scripture tells us that we are God's workmanship, and that he created work for us to do. We believe that purpose is in our DNA. When we help young people understand their identity from that perspective, they resonate with that.

Q: What recommendations do you have for the business leader who's committed to mentoring, coaching, and developing their emerging leaders?

Phyllis: To influence millennials you must relationally connect with them, investing time in forming close and meaningful relationships. They want to know their leaders. This is different from the way that older generations have grown up, where you didn't get to know your leaders or boss. These millennials want to know what they think and if they are being genuine.

Q: Great insight. What other recommendations?

Phyllis: Authenticity is critical. They are constantly looking for real, credible, trustworthy leaders who will help them grow. They want to be mentored by those leaders. They want to watch those leaders. They want to not just hear what they want to say; they want to see what they're doing. They really want to understand.

Q: That's what we're hearing loudly also. Anything else?

Phyllis: Give them opportunities to catch what you're doing and learn from it. They want to be near their leader. We often talk about things that are caught as opposed to being taught, and I think that is very true for millennials. So, as leaders, if you have millennials on your team, you have to invest time. They want to watch you as you live authentically.

There are 75 million millennials in the United States, and by 2025 they will comprise over 75 percent of the workforce. It's a huge investment for leaders to take this most educated, connected, and studied generation and help them know how to live their lives in a way that will be impactful in the world.

Q: Where can we find other resources, Phyllis?

Phyllis: Three sample lessons of our twelve-lesson online series are available when you type *Lead Like Jesus* + *Igniting Influence* into your browser. Included in each session are a three-to five-minute video, a short article with great stats and quotes, specific examples of Jesus and his leadership, case studies of Biblical principles applied to today, and challenging discussion questions to help emerging leaders grow.

Sisu is a grim, gritty, white-knuckle form of courage that is typically presented in situations where success is against the odds. It expresses itself in taking action against the odds and displaying courage and resoluteness in the face of adversity. In other words, it is deciding on a course of action and then sticking to that decision even despite repeated failures.

—Wikipedia

Part 2

■ ■ ■ ■ ■ ■

Strengthen
Your *Sisu* Spirit

Definition: A resilient resolve that sparks creativity
so that one experiences confident
momentum toward goals.

Sisu
(see'-soo) noun

18

The *Sisu* Spirit
and Leadership

If you have Finnish ancestry like me, chances are you have heard the word *sisu*. It is a five-hundred-year-old Finnish word packed with meaning. In short, it means an unconditional commitment to pursuing one's goals, regardless of the obstacles (note the word *unconditional*).

People from Finland first arrived in the United States in the mid-nineteenth century. Their main reasons for emigrating included unemployment, low wages, and wanting to avoid military service in the Russian Army. Finns left their homeland looking for better opportunities; however, homesteading proved difficult and required an extra measure of hardiness and determination. It required a *sisu* spirit.

Experts say that there's no word in the English language that can fully express what *sisu* means. It's about the internal strength, unapologetic perseverance, unwavering determination, and relentless courage to be proactive. It's beyond mental toughness.

Because this word is part of my heritage and my childhood, I felt incredibly validated when the International Positive Psychology Association proclaimed 2015 as "The Year of *Sisu*." To celebrate, the association interviewed Emilia Lahti, who's working toward her PhD on *sisu*. Emilia says, "At its core is the idea that there is more strength to us than what often meets the eye. *Sisu* means to exceed yourself, take action against slim odds, and transform barriers into frontiers. It's the action mind-set of eating small nuisances for breakfast and diving into the storm even when there is no silver lining in sight. It is the 'second wind' of mental toughness, after the individual has reached the limits of their observed mental or physical capacities."[1] The concept has been covered and celebrated by *Forbes*, *Business Insider*, and *Scientific American*.

The Perseverance and Accountability Leadership Framework

Leaders who possess a *sisu* spirit sign up for seemingly impossible tasks. They step out despite their fears and take action against long odds. They step up when they're faced with obstacles, knowing there is more strength than what meets the eye. They reach deep within in order to stretch their comfort zone. So instead of just thinking that everything will turn out okay, a person with *sisu* spirit has the conviction that they will be all right, and they will take the necessary actions to shape those outcomes, whether they have a Finnish heritage or not. These creative leaders possess both high perseverance and high accountability for their own actions. They have resilience. They have confidence. They have *sisu*.

Others forfeit personal power, including ingenuity and strength. It's disheartening to see young leaders with promise who aren't reaching their full potential because this quality is underdeveloped. They have the talent and skills. They know the ball is in their court to create momentum, but they don't make the needed changes. They lack commitment to do anything different. There's no fire in the belly, no get-up-and-go. They desire to be successful, but they aren't going to alter their actions to achieve the success, regardless of what anyone says or does.

In our sales recruiting practice, we never recommend hiring candidates who lack unconditional commitment to being successful. It's a red flag on the sales assessment findings, especially if they're tasked with going after new business. They're prone to let their emotions of fear and discomfort take precedence over what they know they should be doing to crack a new account or tackle new markets. They typically won't take the risks to reach out to the correct decision maker or to ask penetrating business-appropriate questions that will disrupt the status quo and earn the business.

The most difficult workers for us to deal with are those with intense perseverance but low personal accountability. They are relentless in blaming others as *the* problem and don't see themselves as part of the problem or the solution. For some, this subversive attitude is observed in one-on-one conversations, and they keep this poison to themselves. Others are energized by spreading the poison. Some do this in their one-on-one interactions with their colleagues. Others, especially those who have good communication skills, will be overt in recruiting people to their perspective. They aggressively feed unsuspecting followers their illusion of "can't."

Then there are silent complainers who do nothing at all with their lives. They have both low perseverance and accountability. They play the victim role flawlessly and silently blame others for everything. It's always someone else's fault.

Millennials and *Sisu*

In our recent Millennial Matters survey, 17 percent of business leaders responded that one of their top concerns is millennials' lack of accountability, 13 percent were concerned with their lack of determination, and 9 percent were concerned with their lack of resiliency and ability to bounce back.

The blame game never works. When a person chooses to shift blame, they completely discard their creativity and genius. They maintain focus on what can't be done versus what can be done.

In our coaching and development of sales professionals, we use a validated assessment tool that's based on research done on more than a million salespeople. The accountability findings are spot-on. We use the tool both for helping companies recruit the right sales professionals with strong sales potential and for developing their existing staff.

Historically, we've seen about 60 percent of all sales professionals—from entry level to sales managers to VPs of sales—have a tendency to point to other people or circumstances when they don't hit their sales targets, rather than take personal responsibility for their results. Surprisingly, we're finding that younger salespeople are half as likely to externalize when losing a sale. Why is this surprising? Because many label this generation the entitlement generation. We don't know what's causing this trend in younger salespeople. Are they the first hump that Dennis Thum talked about?

Even though there's a trend that we're observing, the issue still needs addressing. In partnering with company leaders to hire and retain top talent, we find that 100 percent of top-tier new-business developers and rainmakers take personal accountability for their actions and behaviors. They recognize that they have the capacity to be creative innovators who can solve problems. They have a strong *sisu* spirit.

A WORD FROM A MILLENNIAL ...

"In my experience, millennials crave feedback, both positive and constructive. We need to know when we are on track and when we are off track. That is helpful and it's respectful. I have reported to many different leaders, and I have felt most inclined to work hard for the leaders I have had who truly demonstrate the respect they have for me and my skills. They have been clear in communicating their expectations of me—and gently encouraging me when I'm off track. When I have felt that my leader genuinely values my thoughts and efforts when they give me something to work on, I've felt more motivated to do a good job. Remember, we grew up with a lot of pressure to excel academically to the point where a lot of us missed out on developing other skills."

What is our role as seasoned business leaders who are in either formal or informal mentoring relationships with young leaders? *Sisu* is not just a word but a way of life, and I am passionate about strengthening it in the next generation of leaders. It is an action-enabling strength with the capacity to:

- inspire young leaders to step out of their comfort zones;
- stimulate young leaders to stretch their mental reserves and preconceived resources;
- propel young leaders to push through their mental, emotional, and physical barriers;
- set young leaders apart from many of their colleagues who give up too early; and
- provide a competitive edge in any endeavor.

Experienced business leaders are instrumental in encouraging future leaders to surround themselves with people who will strengthen their *sisu* spirit. Let's commit to nurturing this character quality in our next-gen leaders.

Mental toughness is built one battle at a time. A key to fostering *sisu* in your emerging leader is you, the experienced business leader, who comes alongside to share wisdom, insight and discernment. With your support, your up-and-coming leader develops the stamina that's needed for flourishing in their professional and personal lives. You help them get the leadership momentum needed to lead well for the long haul. And it's our hope that they'll also empower leaders in their spheres of influence.

Sisu is more than just a Finnish word. It's a philosophy and a way of life. Raising this character strength will pay back dividends for many years to come.

LEADERSHIP LESSON

To spark creativity and tap brilliance,
resolve to live every day with a *sisu* spirit.

19

Develop a Disciplined Action Mind-set

Have you ever confidently made a decision only to find later it was the worst decision of your life?

I know firsthand what that feels like. I bought Trail Rider, a snowmobile sleigh manufacturing business. We built and distributed a tow-behind for snowmobile enthusiasts who might want to take their children, pets, and supplies with them on their winter adventures. This business was outside my typical business interests—the innovative, high-tech worlds of Xerox and medical devices. But I was still confident that it would meet our family's long-term needs.

Of course, the success of this business thrives on the presence of snow, of which there is usually plenty. However, the winter following this business transaction marked the arrival of El Niño ... and no snow. It was one of the longer El Niños, lasting several years. Not nearly enough snowmobiling, or any other winter sport that depended on snowfall, happened year after year. It was a total disaster. The financials were bleak. I hated the business.

What did I do?

I played the blame game. I pointed my finger at everybody else. I blamed my husband for persuading me to get into the business, even though I made the final decision. I blamed customers for not buying the product. I even blamed God for not providing the snowfall needed for my business venture.

Timely for me, I was reading a series of books on the importance of accountability processes in building high-performance sales teams. I thought I was helping my teams, but the message was really targeted directly to me. The authors triggered me to apply a disciplined approach, an action mind-set, and an ownership orientation. I needed to draw on my *sisu* spirit to get myself out of the messy circumstance. I couldn't blame my husband, the customers, or God any longer.

In retrospect, my previous viewpoint had been myopic thinking, especially considering El Niño was a global phenomenon and didn't affect only my business and my life. Did any of the blaming solve my problems? No, not at all. Were they appropriate places of blame? No, they weren't.

What resources, coaches, or mentors influenced you to apply an action mind-set and take ownership of the results of your choices?

Millennials and the Action Mind-set

Television, newspapers, blogs, social media posts, and comment sections all seem to focus on identifying problems and pointing fingers. Millennials, just like the rest of us, are quick to jump in and join the chorus. It's easy to join another grumbler when we let our guard down. Unfortunately, that's in the fabric of our culture.

This trend is creating a group of up-and-coming leaders who may lack the resiliency needed to be successful in the long run. Imagine the loss of opportunity if you have a team that spends too much time recovering from setbacks versus climbing back on the horse that threw them and charging after their goals.

A WORD FROM A MILLENNIAL ...

"These statements are made by many gen Xers and baby boomers. They are offensive and untrue. Parents need to accept the responsibility for how they raised their children. It is beyond me why a parent would ever call their child 'self-absorbed' and not do anything to change it. We are 'lazy' because we don't do things according to the way the older generation does things. We are 'ungrateful' because we inherited a world that tells us no matter how hard we work, it will not qualify as the 'American Dream.' We are 'entitled' because we feel as though we deserve more from life but were not taught the tools to achieve it. We are 'self-absorbed' because our parents gave us trophies and never taught us what it feels like to lose. The formative years of our generation were marked by the most rapidly growing technological advancement in history, which has had a profound effect on each us of personally. Millennials may seem self-absorbed because of how we act on social media, but when it comes to global responsibility, our values overwhelmingly reflect social inclusion. The problem is we feel like there is nothing we can do to change the world. We need help to know where to start."

Resilient employees are more willing to deal with disappointment, find creative alternatives, and take calculated risks when they don't succeed. Those who resist wallowing in defeat and get back into the game quickly will emerge as respected leaders.

Your Next-Gen Leader and the Action Mind-set

In our work with sales teams, we know that real growth and change, either personal or professional, will not occur until the excuse-making stops and everyone on the team, including leaders, takes responsibility for moving toward a solution.

So, how might you stimulate your next-gen leader to become more disciplined in taking responsibility and moving forward? Here are some areas where you can work with them to strengthen their leadership influence.

Start Recognizing Excuses

Improve your young leader's ability to recognize excuses. Excuses can be difficult to identify, since the thought process is so prevalent and pervasive within our culture. We think that we're either reporting or hearing the facts, when it's really just our interpretation of reality. We are prone to believe our story. It's difficult to admit, but our interpretation may be faulty. All the way back to the garden of Eden, blaming someone or something else for our misfortunes has been a natural human tendency. In the sales world, excuses typically fall into the following categories:

- "My prospects and clients just don't get it."
- "The industry or market is growing too fast or too slow."
- "The competitors are cutting prices or not playing fair."
- "My boss isn't competent."
- "The other departments aren't doing their jobs."

Once leaders train their ear to hear externalizing, either from themselves or from others, they will be amazed at the endless list of excuses they'll spot.

Stop Accepting Excuses from Themselves

This can be a difficult decision to make because it requires your up-and-coming leader to be intentional and proactive in transforming their own thinking. To achieve both their short-term goals and long-term dreams and aspirations, they need productive thinking that sounds like the following:

- "I take full responsibility for my actions and behaviors."
- "I don't waste time complaining and blaming others."
- "I create action plans that move me forward in achieving my goals."

- "I have the creative resources to deal with any obstacles that comes my way."

Stop Accepting Excuses from Others

Equally as difficult for your mentee is to stop accepting excuses from their friends, peers, coworkers, and managers. They can spark others to start taking responsibility by responding to excuses with a question we train business and sales leaders to use: "If you couldn't use that as an excuse, what might you have done differently to overcome that obstacle and get your desired result?"

This question might sound harsh. Role play with your mentee ways to ask a similar question that feels comfortable for them, based on their personality and behavior style. The goal is for them to have the courage to ask a pertinent, business-appropriate question while keeping a positive relationship intact.

Remind your up-and-coming leader that their goal is to empower others to use their own ingenuity to develop new ways of tackling obstacles and roadblocks. In addition, their commitment to the solution will be much stronger as they come up with the answer themselves.

Anticipate Pushback

To the "What might you have done differently?" approach, we'd love for recipients to respond, "Thanks so much for asking that question. You're correct. I've been waiting for you to confront my thinking patterns." Well, that rarely happens. What does happen? Pushback. People may get defensive or argumentative.

Prepare your next-gen leader to be mentally and emotionally prepared to deal with this response. Practice active listening with them. Train them to recognize that the response from team members is likely to be one of two responses: "Yes, I'm on board," or "No, your idea stinks." Craft a talk track for either response.

Execution: The Discipline of Getting Things Done by Larry Bossidy and Ram Charan is still one of my favorite books. I love what they write about facts and realism: "Leaders need to insist on realism. Yes, people naturally play the blame game, try to hide mistakes, pretend to have a solution when they are clueless, seek to avoid confrontations, and see their side of the story as the only side. However, long-term success in every endeavor is based on getting to the facts, not Pollyanna hopes or wild accusations."[1]

Lend a hand to your next-gen leader as they improve their skills in deciphering the facts, both in themselves as well as in who they live with and work with. As a trusted resource, you have the opportunity to be a mirror for them, gently reflecting what you're hearing from them and whether or not they're blaming others, including customers, colleagues, cultural dynamics, or even God, for their current circumstances.

LEADERSHIP LESSON

Develop an action mind-set to be
a solutions provider, not just a problem identifier.

20

Use the Catalytic Question

"I need help," said the discouraged voice over the phone. "We've invested in new robotics equipment to improve our efficiencies. We have significantly enhanced our capabilities. But we need sales—now. Can you help me shift the sales team into high gear?"

As we talked further, Ron, the president of a mid-sized precision manufacturing company, also admitted that margins were shrinking on even their best accounts. However, his most pressing concern was that they were stuck, having zero success in cracking new accounts and tapping markets.

To search for the root cause of what was stalling growth, we conducted our sales audit. We scrutinized their sales strategies, systems, processes, and people. We dug through everything: the quality of the pipeline, potential issues they might have with hiring criteria, the effectiveness of sales management, and whether the salespeople were even capable of executing the growth strategy. We need to know all this before starting any project so we have clarity about what to focus on first. When I say everything, I mean everything—including leadership.

What did we find? Ron, even though he was forward thinking in upgrading production capabilities, had a victim-oriented mind-set in sales. And he wasn't the only one in the company with this mind-set. His executive team and teams were blaming the competitors for outselling them, the industry for being too global, the company for their weak marketing effort, and their customer service team for being unresponsive to client complaints. He was inadvertently falling into the trap of believing them and passing this negative energy onto the sales team.

To shift the sales team into high gear to land new accounts, Ron needed to change his mind-set and start asking catalytic questions.

Millennials and the Catalytic Question

Millennials are often described as a "hopeful" generation. But being hopeful doesn't guarantee they'll be able to deal with obstacles and rebound quickly.

Their hopeful mind-set is often linked to their ability to dream big and to expect that they can get whatever they want from life. That can be a great mind-set to have—if it goes hand in hand with the reality of what it takes to achieve those dreams. This reality calls for intense resilience, the grim, gritty, white-knuckle form of courage that is typically presented in situations where success is against the odds. Do you think most millennial leaders are equipped to deal with the daunting difficulties they face?

While mentoring next-gen leaders, I sometimes find that they seem scared of the action they have to take. In response to the fear, they procrastinate, make lists, do online research, write out plans, and make more lists. They appear to be extremely busy, without moving forward on what really matters. And as the deadline approaches or the project becomes overdue, little has been done. They find themselves intensely stressed, wishing they'd started executing their plans sooner.

The difference between successful and unsuccessful leaders is often just the ability to gain traction and get something done, regardless of any curveballs being thrown at them. The successful ones usually aren't smarter, more gifted, or more talented than anyone else. They simply don't get distracted by the naysayers, and they don't get discouraged by their own inner critics. They work harder, longer, and smarter until they reach their goals.

A WORD FROM A MILLENNIAL …

"I think people of my generation have been protected and given a *lot*. We've been given so much that it takes a moment of realization to come to the conclusion that nobody is going to give you anything. You have to fight for what you want and to avoid complacency."

Your Next-Gen Leader and the Catalytic Question

This catalytic question, introduced in the previous chapter, stimulates others to focus on what they can do, not on what they can't do: "If you couldn't use that excuse, what might you do to tackle the obstacles and roadblocks and get the results you want?" It unlocks creativity. Action-oriented or excuse-busting questions nurture the personal responsibility needed for high performance in any role at work or home.

Use these four simple but effective steps to increase your next-gen leader's ability to be a positive catalytic problem-solver and solution provider.

Nurture an Ownership Mind-set

Guide your mentee to apply an ownership mind-set, where they take inventory of their own input, behavior, activities, and contributions to a situation. Remind them of the following:

- They can only control their behavior. They can't control outcomes.
- They need to watch their input and be highly intentional in what they're listening to, reading, and saying. Is it positive and constructive?
- To be countercultural and to be a leader in accountability, they need to be highly intentional about their input.

Be an Innovator

Be a catalyst for them, using your business and leadership acumen to inspire them to do the following:

- Craft three to four possible solutions to a current problem they have. Then work with them to explore the possible consequences and ramifications of each of those possible solutions.
- Solicit insight from others to strengthen these ideas even further.
- Leverage the power of "might." *Might* is a powerful word in a catalyst question. It invites possibilities, options, and new connections. An article in the *Harvard Business Review*, "The Secret Phrase Top Innovators Use," underscores the impact of this word. "The 'how might we' approach innovation ensures that would-be innovators are asking the right questions and using the best wording. Proponents of this increasingly popular practice say it's surprisingly effective—and that it can be seen as a testament to the power of language in helping to spark creative thinking and freewheeling collaboration."[1]

Take Action

Surging forward is critical to being a solution provider. Strengthen your young leader's clarity with an action plan that has concrete next steps. For some, a long-term action plan can be overwhelming. If that is the case, assist them to chart at least one measurable action step. Work with your young leader so they get increasing clarity on how to resolve an issue with each step they take.

You may also need to guide them to prioritize their to-do list and focus on the most important actions needed to move forward, not just the easiest steps. Spur them to be the first to offer a suite of solutions and to have an innovation mind-set.

Stretch Every Day

Advocate that your future leader stretch their comfort zone every day. Yes, every day. It's easy to jot an action item on the to-do list. It is more daunting to actually do the item so that you can check it off as complete.

When I'm working with next-gen leaders, I regularly ask them where they stretched themselves in the last day or the last week. Where did they stretch their comfort zone by asking a new question? Where did they practice a new concept? Who did they talk to, even if they were afraid to talk to them?

When your mentee reports their courage, celebrate. They're actively embracing their growth. They are taking action in the face of fear. When they can do this on a consistent basis, they can know their future will be packed with an ever-growing suite of leadership opportunities.

Every time your next-gen leader sweats, their comfort zone expands and they grow in their capacity as a leader.

A WORD FROM A MILLENNIAL …

"It would be interesting to hear from our mentors about which mind-set is the most difficult for them."

By asking catalyst questions for a given situation, we all have the potential to apply an action-oriented mind-set, just like Ron. Support your next-gen leader in their journey to develop a *sisu* spirit, a mind-set that overcomes roadblocks and keeps them from falling into the victim mentality that pervades our society.

LEADERSHIP LESSON

An action-oriented mind-set helps us
overcome the obstacles in our lives.

21

Be the
Domino Difference

The power of the domino amazes me. It must impress other people too, since the YouTube video "Domino Chain Reaction (Short Version)" has more than two million views.[1] It's presented by Stephen Morris, and based on the original idea Lorne Whitehead described in the *American Journal of Physics* in 1983.

The narrator demonstrates how one domino can knock over another domino about 1.5 times larger than itself. Based on the flow of mechanical energy, if you start a chain with a miniature domino five millimeters high and one millimeter thick, how many dominos would it take for that last domino to be as tall as the Empire State Building? Only twenty-nine dominos. In just thirty moves, a miniature domino that's only five millimeters high—less than a quarter of an inch—can topple the Empire State Building.

If one domino has that much impact, how much impact can we have?

Which of your mentors have had a positive domino effect on you? Which leaders had a negative effect?

Millennials and the Domino Difference

Millennials react badly to a negative workplace vibe. They were raised to believe they are special, and they still want to feel that way in the workplace.

One of the positive outcomes of this mind-set, as I mentioned previously, is that millennials welcome feedback when they're on track and doing things well. Not the kind of feedback that we remember as a quarterly or annual performance review, but daily feedback on how they're doing.

On the flip side, they may have a tendency to get defensive when told they are doing poorly. Be strategic and respectful when giving them feedback that can get them moving in the right direction.

A WORD FROM A MILLENNIAL ...

"I know of many brilliant world-renowned experts in their field who are not respected by millennials because the person is rude or condescending to them. We feel their negative dominos and respond to them accordingly."

Young leaders desire to be part of something bigger than just the job they were hired to do. They want to be part of a team of dominos that can topple Empire-State-Building-sized problems together. Thus, they not only enjoy the company they work for, they also want to be part of its decision-making processes.

They want their voices heard. They want their voices to matter.

How might we nurture our next-gen leaders to embrace the power of positive (or negative) impact that's available in every move they make?

Your Next-Gen Leader
and the Domino Difference

So, how do you mentor your next-gen leader to be wise about the domino effects of their words, actions, and priorities, even when they feel their actions are as insignificant as a domino that's less than a quarter of an inch tall?

One of the resources I keep on my "best-of-the-best leadership book shelf" is *A Failure of Nerve: Leadership in the Age of the Quick Fix* by Edwin H. Friedman. He spotlights the importance of a leader's ability to be self-differentiated. Self-differentiation focuses on two primary areas that leaders need to work on strengthening:

- Their ability to distinguish between emotions and thinking, and to be able to access their insights proactively versus reactively
- Their capacity not to get wrapped up in other people's emotions

Your committed support of working with your next-gen leader to clearly define the difference between their own thinking and the other person's emotions and thinking is monumental in developing their leadership capacity. In fine-tuning this ability, they will be able to stay in a positive relationship with others, while still maintaining their individuality. Their influence will expand as they develop the reputation of maintaining a calm, steady presence, even in the midst of chaos.

Your committed support of your next-gen leader as they grow in these areas will be monumental in developing their leadership capacity. Yes, some of these tips are repeats. They are worth repeating. They are the domino difference.

Put a Stake in the Ground

The more clarity your next-gen leader has on who they are (their gifts, strengths, principles, and unique perspectives), what their values are, and the goals they are pursuing in life, the more adept they will be at standing firm. They will have put their stake in the ground so that everyone knows where they stand. This firmness gives others a clear vision of where they are, inviting others to provide clarity about where *they* are.

Resist the BAND-AID™ Approach

In the heat of the moment, your next-gen leader may be tempted to cave into pressure, either individual or group pressure, to implement a quick-fix BAND-AID™ solution. Stick close to them and walk through strategies on how not to succumb. Be the sounding board to help them set aside the chaotic, intense emotions so they can calmly reflect on what they're seeing, hearing, and learning. The solution will undoubtedly be a longer-term fix.

Iron Sharpens Iron

The best ideas are often forged in the crucible of opposite ideas blended together in the heat of discussion. Map out strategies to help your next-gen leader strengthen the relationship capital of those they're dealing with. They can still build a collaborative working relationship with others, even amid intense disagreement.

Fix the Process, Not the People

Over the years, we've ascertained that you can't fix people, only the process. However, your up-and-coming leader may not know the truth of this principle. Every person has their own set of abilities, as well as their own weaknesses and warts.

As leaders, we have learned that the problem people bring to us, the presenting problem, is never the real problem. It's a symptom. Remind your leader of this fact and that it takes a lot of digging to find the root cause, the core issue.

Focus on fixing the process so that a creative long-term solution can be developed, in spite of the people.

Track and Recognize a "No"

Many young leaders I know take a "no" personally. Invite your mentee to make a game of getting a no, or getting rejected.

Invite them to track the number of times they get a no, or feel like they get rejected, in a day or week. The traditional mantra in the selling world is that it takes five nos to get a yes. Today, we often have to go for ten nos in order to get a yes—maybe more. So guide your mentee as they develop mental toughness.

Whether it's in sales or in leadership, the pathway will be filled with nos. Some of the nos will be the straightforward, in-your-face type. Others will be more evasive—that is, they don't return your phone call, e-mails, or texts. Still other nos will be sugary, some almost to the point of warm marshmallow goo: they'll tell you how wonderful you are, and that maybe in the future they'll consider your idea. But it's really a no.

Help your young leader discern the yeses from the nos. Then assist them to craft a go-forward plan, based on the information and insights they've been gathering along the way. At times they'll need your expertise to know when to celebrate their victories and when to cut their losses. There's a saying in sales: "Some will. Some won't. So what? What's next?" It's a mantra worth exercising.

How does the domino difference relate to a *sisu* spirit? Here's how I see it. It takes a "grim, gritty, white-knuckle form of courage" to choose to differentiate yourself and take a stand that's different from what everyone is telling you. That's what Ron had to do—put the *sisu* domino in action.

LEADERSHIP LESSON

Create a positive impact
by being the domino difference.

Dear Reader,

What an imprint you are leaving on the hearts and minds of next-gen leaders! They have a deep desire to make a difference, to be world-changers. Through your consistent and wise mentoring, you're supporting them through some of the most important changes they will ever make.

This pathway to acquire, strengthen, and leverage their leadership tools helps them to be catalysts for innovation. They will be countercultural, withstanding intense pressure to conform to a victim-oriented culture. Their resilient resolve will spark creativity and innovation for every endeavor they choose to engage in. As a result, there will be confident momentum toward personal, business, and community goals.

You're building a leader who's resilient, mentally tough, with a *sisu* spirit.

> *"When you're in over your head, I'll be there with you.*
> *When you're in rough waters, you will not go down.*
> *When you're between a rock and a hard place,*
> *it won't be a dead end."*
> ISAIAH 43:2

—Danita

Interview with Rocky LaGrone, CEO of Effective Sales Development

As part of an international coalition of sales development experts, I have access to a whole range of resources who call themselves "experts." However, only a select few actually get on my list of Dantotsu sales development firms. Rocky is one of them. His sales, management and leadership strategies are proven and practical. He sees clearly amidst confusion and chaos and he helps his clients do the same.

Q: Tell us about yourself and your purpose at Effective Sales Development.

Rocky: Our purpose is to build world-class sales teams and help our fellow man improve the quality of their life and the lives of those around them.

Q: What are some of the biggest problems you see in sales teams today?

Rocky: Overall, I see sales teams that aren't properly managed or measured. They're not motivated effectively, and they are not held truly accountable. They are not coached on a regular schedule and therefore flounder to mediocrity. Sales teams don't have clear achievable goals that are married with their personal goals, so they don't produce enough new business. There is typically no sales process to guide the salesperson or to provide a coaching vehicle for sales management.

Q: Rocky, as you're working with business owners, what are some of the problems that you're seeing as they relate to developing sales and leadership talent in millennials?

Rocky: There are three very specific things that have happened in the last ten years that have changed the selling world and make it difficult for business owners to grow revenue through their sales departments. The first is that the impact of 9/11 changed the idea of working for the almighty dollar to working more for a cause and a quality of life. In the United States, 9/11 brought about a pause. People realized that life is short, and the importance of family and friends came into focus. Work-life balance became the mantra, and it was adopted by millennials.

The second observation is that technology has made great advances. Rapid advancements of available information for buyers via the Internet have allowed for a cultural shift in sales to bring what would have been an outside sales position to an inside position. Add to that what is now dubbed Inbound Marketing and we have an entirely new sales landscape.

Q: What's the biggest impact you're seeing from this trend in sales?

Rocky: The buyer is showing up much farther down the path and is much more educated. Millennials fill this new role in sales function as long as they remain patient with the buyer. The challenge is with communication and persuasion skills. Because they have embraced technology their whole lives, they don't always anticipate the buyer's questions. They sell themselves, their employers, their products, their services, and their prospects short. They don't always understand why it's critical to ask better and more questions to ensure the buyers are considering the right products and services.

Q: Helpful insights, Rocky. And what's the third trend?

Rocky: Millennials were raised by baby boomers and gen Xers. They were coddled over inclusion and achievement without effort. They were over-protected with safety, rules, regulations, helicopter parenting, and the promise of another trophy. That created instant gratification, risk aversion, and team performance over individual acceleration.

Millennials are very concerned about life-work balance, and they're motivated by personal time. They want to contribute to making the world a better place for their future and for generations to come. They're motivated by being part of a team and by being part of something bigger than themselves. They want a positive working environment that is environmentally friendly.

Q: Motivation is an important part of sales. How does all this impact motivation?

Rocky: Millennial motivation is intrinsic, not extrinsic. We have access to Objective Management Group's database with well over one million salespeople that have been evaluated. In just the last five years, we've seen an exact dynamic flip in the motivation measurements that are identified. Today, we find that 78 percent of the people in sales that we evaluate are intrinsically motivated compared to five years ago when 78 percent of the people were extrinsically motivated. Employers who understand this will have an extreme advantage. It's kind of like the old saying: "If we know what the rules of the game are, we know how to win the game." One of the biggest challenges for seasoned business leaders is that the rules have changed.

Q: And how does this all tie into accountability, which is an important part of any sales team?

Rocky: There must be more clarity with focus on the reward and the positive outcome. Just like everybody else, millennials have to be held accountable, but the way you go about doing that is very different. If you really try to hold them accountable with repercussions and consequences, they have a tendency to shut down. Communicating specific expectations is key. In reality, you can make a really simple change by making the measurements clear up-front. There are no surprises when you say, "Here's what you're going to be measured on. Here's when you're going to be measured. Here's how you're going to be rewarded when you meet or exceed those expectations."

Q: If you were to summarize some of the key ideas for business owners and leaders who are looking to raise the bar on leading, managing, coaching, and mentoring millennials, what would be your top three recommendations?

Rocky:

1. Don't assume that everyone in the millennial marketplace has a *sisu* spirit.

2. It's your job to figure out how to pull it out of them.

3. Don't give up too early.

Q: Thanks for those insights, Rocky. Where can our readers reach you?

Rocky: They can reach me at SalesDevelopmentExpert.com. And they should make certain that they tell me that Danita sent them. You have a helpful way of recommending concrete action steps. So I am interested in hearing how they are beginning to be implemented. Plus, I'm interested in their hopes for tapping the unique talents and skills of the millennials on their teams.

Section 3

Engage with Collaboration

You can change your world
by changing your words. …
Remember, death and life are
in the power of the tongue.

—Joel Osteen

Part 1

Respect Relationship Wiring

Definition: A valuing of the uniqueness of both self
and others that fuels collaboration
so that teamwork is maximized.

22

Relationship Wiring and Leadership

"There's a prairie fire!" Dad exclaimed.

I stopped walking and searched the late-night horizon. I saw very little except the stars of the Milky Way scattered brilliantly across the sky. Mom and Dad were already racing to our stash of rakes and gunnysacks, so I quickly followed. We tossed the tools and sacks into the pickup, along with buckets of water. Then we drove at high speed on loose gravel roads toward the fire.

As we got closer, I could see the smoke. A wall of fire was leaping across our neighbor's wheat field when we pulled up. Two dozen or more neighbors ferociously beat at the fire with their own water-soaked gunnysacks. Some people were black with smoke and coughing. Exhausted, they kept fighting, and we joined them. Thankfully, the rural fire department arrived before we collapsed from weariness and smoke inhalation.

Even today I'm amazed that my dad spotted the small speck of a fire in the distance, when all I saw was blackness. How did he see it? He has the sharp eyes of an eagle, and he knew that a prairie fire could devastate an entire community. To thrive, or even survive in these rural areas, we needed to be on the lookout for hazards that could devastate both our holdings as well as our neighbor's property.

Success is not for the solitary cowboy bravely riding out to save the ranch. Success is based on all of us working together toward common goals. It requires valuing the unique contribution we each bring to the table, as well as respecting what others bring. This fuels communication and collaboration.

Collaborative relationships are needed for fulfilling lives, both personally and professionally.

Honoring Both Self and Others

Leaders who have a healthy self-image, and who honor and respect others, maximize teamwork. These leaders help their teams to confidently communicate and collaborate, building healthy, trusted relationships. This dynamic produces synergistic participation.

When an effective leader brings individuals together, they create a climate where the end result is greater than the sum of their individual efforts. They know their own expertise, while recognizing the insights and perspectives of others on the project. So, it's a "1 + 1 = 3 outcome." Or, it could even be a "1 + 1 = 99 result." The team is stronger when working together.

Think of a V-formation of geese. When I see the familiar pattern in the sky, I'm reminded that it's the leader who creates synergistic collaboration.

What are the advantages of geese working together versus each trying to make the long flight on its own? First, a group effort conserves the energy of each bird. Each goose flies behind and a little higher than the bird in front of him, so each takes advantage of the partial windbreak and doesn't tire as easily. Second, each bird takes a turn flying at the front of the V, giving over the lead position when it gets tired. This way, the geese can go for an extended time before they need to rest.

That is similar to relationship wiring, which is valuable to understand. Relationship wiring is the uniqueness of both self and others that fuels collaboration so that teamwork is maximized.

Unfortunately, some leaders in all generations have strong personas but don't value the perspectives, insights, and experience others bring to the table. They have gifts and talents and good ideas, but because they don't collaborate with others, their ideas seldom become great ideas. Sure, other teammates can talk about their ideas, but they already know whose idea will win. Over time, such personas shut down team communication and squelch creativity. People stop contributing because their ideas don't make a difference anyway. These lone-wolf leaders rarely create the momentum needed to bring outstanding results.

Other leaders are incredibly talented but struggle with low self-image. This type of leader often harbors resentment toward their bosses. The sad truth about these leaders is they feel better about themselves if they're able to please everyone else. This means they tend to spread themselves so thin that they have little energy left to give wing to their own ideas and solutions.

They do not honor both self and others. They have poor relationship wiring.

What are you doing to help your millennials develop healthy self-images so they can act with confidence but still see the importance of collaboration?

Millennials and Their Relationship Wiring

Millennials grew up in a relatively impersonal world, and also saturated with technology. Technology is how they make new "friends," look for jobs, and buy things. Most everything happens online, not in person.

The limitations of technology-based communication were revealed in our Millennial Matters survey. Only 11 percent of millennial participants listed lack of verbal communication skills as their top concern. Only 8 percent listed low conflict-resolution skills as top. For seasoned leaders, this de-socialization of America is creating significant workplace complications as we attempt to cross the growing generational and cultural divides.

A WORD FROM A MILLENNIAL …

"I don't know if the two necessarily need to go hand in hand. While I would think that a lot of the ways that millennials interact are less personal than the 'older generation' (most of us would *much* rather text than call someone), I think many of us also think that growing up in this age of technology has helped us get more connected in other ways. I even remember growing up and using the giant phone in our car (almost the size of a shoe box) that let us stay in contact with family while we were on the road. I stay in contact with more of my high school friends with Facebook than I could ever dream of doing without. These aren't deep, meaningful relationships by any means, but they're relationships nonetheless. These relationships, which seem so superficial compared to face-to-face, are something to think about!"

Do you remember the original *Star Trek* series? (One of my all-time favorite heroes was Captain Kirk.) Not even the most innovative movie producer or prop department from that era could envision the "futuristic" gadgets that are now part of almost every household in America.

These technologies influence the way millennials are wired relationally. As Steve Wilkens and Mark L. Sanford discuss in *Hidden Worldviews: Eight Cultural Stories That Shape Our Lives*, a myriad of worldviews is subtly and subconsciously being promoted in today's culture:

- Individualism: Use all available resources to free yourself from the limiting expectations of others. Be yourself.
- Consumerism: Accumulate more and more stuff to meet all your needs, even your emotional and spiritual needs.
- Postmodern Tribalism: Overcome (perceived) oppression from (perceived) dominant groups via political activism, in order to establish your identity.
- Relativism: Free yourself from judgments imposed by anyone other than yourself.[1]

A WORD FROM A MILLENNIAL ...

"It seems that the four of these worldviews feed into each other as well. Individualism leads to the desire to buy things that help you exert your individuality. Sometimes we intentionally buy eccentric things just to prove that we don't care about what other people think about us (relativism). If someone does judge us, we lash out and attack them (postmodern tribalism)."

This collision of how we view the world can fuel division, when really it could be fueling discussion.

My daughter, whom I deeply admire and respect, recently returned home from a trip to Europe. There she visited many World War II sites while reading Dietrich Bonhoeffer's biography. Both Europe and World War II came alive for her during her stay.

I enjoyed hearing her impressions since I had visited many of the same countries while they were under communist rule in the 1980s. As we discussed her trip, the topic of immigration and refugees came up. Little did I know until this conversation that we have very different perspectives. It was tense for both of us.

Later, while reflecting on our exchange of ideas, I realized that if there's this much angst in discussing a difficult topic between two people who love, care about, and respect each other, then how much more difficult is it for those who don't have good relational wiring?

Many of us think that millennials have participated in so many team projects during their education years that they're adept at handling conflict. This is not so. First, many haven't had enough work experience to know how to function in a true collaboration. In a business realm, it takes conviction to handle a wide range of perspectives and insights coming from the multiple generations currently in the workforce. Second, many of the schools' "team projects" involved collaboration via technology, not face-to-face communication.

A WORD FROM A MILLENNIAL ...

"Almost everyone I know, when asked about working in group projects, hates them. Everyone sees themselves as being the one who carries the team and does all the work. Everyone."

The old command-and-control style of leadership is no longer effective. Encouraging and partnering with people to perform at their best is most effective in the context of a strong relationship where trust is nurtured.

As experienced leaders, we know the power of the team. Relational wiring is a place where you can proactively and positively impact millennials. With your guidance and insight, they can build on their talents and strengths to gain leadership influence and become positive role models for those they lead, both now and in the future.

Work with your mentee on valuing their identity while they also collaborate with the diverse talents of their teammates. By respecting others, we treat them the way they want to be treated, we listen intently to what they are saying, we ask insightful questions, and we deal with difficult conversations.

Collaborative relationships result in a positive updraft for everyone. Teamwork and collaborative problem-solving are maximized, and forward momentum is achieved.

LEADERSHIP LESSON

Transformative mentoring and developing
of a young leader happens in the context
of a strong, trusted relationship.

23

Respect Every Person You Meet

"Let us extend respect to each other, especially when we may disagree."

Unconditional respect, even when we disagree, is becoming a novelty. Because of that, I find myself moved by the words of Secretary of State Rex Tillerson, spoken during his first address to State Department officials: "Lastly, we're going to treat each other with respect. No one will tolerate disrespect of anyone. Before we are employees of the State Department, we are human beings. Let us extend respect to each other, especially when we may disagree."[1] Leaders who treat all people with respect—no matter what their title, income, or political party—are widely admired.

I applied these values when I was national sales manager at Micro-Tech Hearing Instruments. I hired salespeople regularly, and one of my "hidden" interviewers was the receptionist. I could be two thumbs up on a candidate, but if the receptionist said the candidate treated her rudely or disrespectfully, it was an automatic and immediate disqualifier.

Why? Respect. It's that important. No amount of talent or charm makes it worth hiring a disrespectful person. I'm certain my high standards for respect saved me from hiring the wrong person many times.

How did you learn the importance of respecting all people, regardless of their title, income, or position?

Millennials and Respect

Every generation has a unique understanding of respect. Previous generations were raised to respect anyone who was an "elder." However, in the Western world today, we fear the aches, pains, and wrinkles. Getting older is viewed as negative, and we fight it with every possible means.

However, when traveling to places like Africa and China, I see everyone (yes, even millennials) showing the utmost respect to older people. The experiences and wisdom of elders are seen as something to be treasured.

The millennials I mentor approach respect as a two-way street. They tell me that by my respecting them, listening intently to what they say, and asking thoughtful questions, I'm guaranteed of their respect. Even if they're the newest employee in the workplace, they want to be seen as a valuable player on the team, despite the age gap.

This foundation of mutual respect is the place from which they will be open to mentoring. They're more likely to show respect if they can see that it will fly both ways.

A WORD FROM A MILLENNIAL ...

"In my opinion, our generation has a high level of respect for others. This may come as a surprise to most because of our bad reputation, but it is certainly the case when you take a step back. From what I have observed and additionally noticed in myself, we will treat others with the same amount of respect they show us."

In my mentoring work with millennials, I always enjoy discussions on this topic. Here are some of the thoughts they have shared with me:

- "I hate the idea that someone is respected just because he's older than me. If someone treats me with respect and he models a respectable way of life, I will respect him."
- "When my boss is willing to listen to me and hear my ideas, he immediately gets my respect, because he's giving me a chance to show my potential."
- "I know some of my friends can be very disrespectful, not only to older people, but to anyone who disagrees with them. But please, we are *not* all like that."

A WORD FROM A MILLENNIAL ...

"We often hear the phrase 'Business isn't personal.' None of us believe that. In fact, most of us believe that business is the most personal thing you can be a part of. When you aren't in a good and trusting relationship with those around you, your environment becomes toxic. With the ability to go other places, we do. Better yet, we figure out how to start our own company when our thoughts and opinions aren't valued. It may be that they *are* valued, and we just don't perceive them as valued. The best way to *show* us that you value what we have to say isn't by waiting to talk to us at our annual review."

Millennials have been raised without traditional boundaries. They are independent thinkers and often don't even realize when they're being disrespectful. This is where you, the experienced leader, play a vital role. You can model the true meaning of respect in your everyday interactions with them. Respect is usually "caught," not "taught." Be kind and thoughtful to every person you meet, regardless of their role, position, or background. Model respect by talking positively of people who are not present.

A WORD FROM A MILLENNIAL ...

"We may not realize it's disrespectful to interrupt someone when we have a 'brilliant' idea that just can't wait. As a group, we don't value punctuality as much as the previous generation, and we don't think of it as disrespectful. Also, many of us think it's okay to check our iPhone in the middle of a meeting. We might not even think of it as rude."

RESPECT and Your Next-Gen Leader

This acronym RESPECT (React, Encourage, Sensitivity, Politeness, Extraordinary kindness, Considerate, Timeliness) can be a useful guide as you model respect and collaboration with your next-gen leader. RESPECT will help you to develop their collaboration quotient.

React

React positively to the potential talents and strengths you identify in your mentee. They crave positive affirmation. Plus, they thrive on clear communication. Give them direct feedback about their positive traits and the areas where they need to improve.

A WORD FROM A MILLENNIAL ...

"It's deflating when a leader or boss gives great feedback and positive comments about your idea and then does nothing about it. It feels as though they have read a book about listening to us and then they spew a few comments they think we want to hear just to shut us up. If an idea isn't going to be entertained, the respectful thing, in our eyes, is to actually let us know. It's worse to act like we can share things. We see right through that."

Encourage

Encourage respectful listening by creating a safe atmosphere where ideas (even the wacky ones) can be shared. Model good questioning skills as you seek to understand their differing perspectives. Model how to ask deeper-level questions, even when dealing with conflict and controversy. Don't shut down communication with negative labeling. Remind them of Patrick Lencioni's observation: "When there is trust, conflict becomes nothing but the pursuit of truth, an attempt to find the best possible answer."[2]

Sensitivity

Sensitivity to cultural differences is important. I work with people from all around the globe and have experienced that how someone was raised influences how they act. What I perceive as disrespect might mean quite the opposite in a foreign culture. Teach sensitivity, and don't assume disrespect.

Politeness

Politeness means having good manners, which are often neglected in our fast-paced high-tech society. Show respect by getting back to the basics. This starts with saying *please* and *thank you*. Model attentiveness in conversations and meetings. Don't answer or look at your phone when you're in conversation with someone else.

Extraordinary Kindness

Extraordinary kindness makes a big difference. Model kindness to your mentee. Show that you value them by doing something extra. If they aren't anticipating the gesture or kind word, it makes a positive, lasting impact and strengthens mutual respect.

Considerate

Considerate people are given respect. You might think personal or health problems are none of your mentee's business, but personal disclosure helps build trust. When you're willing to be vulnerable, so will they.

Timeliness

Timeliness is a direct reflection of one's character and credibility. When you're running behind schedule, let your next-gen leader know. That shows you respect and value their time. Ask them to do the same.

A two-way mentoring relationship takes time. Motivate your next-gen leader to respect others more genuinely. This will help them to develop strong, collaborative teams both now and for years to come. Respect that goes both ways will add momentum to your business growth and succession strategies. Let's heed Tillerson's charge for our work with millennials: "Let us extend respect to each other, especially when we may disagree." Lead the flock.

LEADERSHIP LESSON

If you want to be respected,
respect others.

24

Practice the Power
of Questions

Sometimes a strength can become a weakness, can't it? While searching for my first job, I inventoried my abilities and decided the most prized skill was my ability to talk. Yes, talk.

Then, in the early years of my sales job, reality struck: a sales job isn't just about talking. It's about listening. In order to listen well, asking the right questions becomes crucial.

I entered the school of hard knocks while learning to ask deeper, more insightful questions. Without getting to the heart of an issue, it's impossible to recommend the best solution to your client. The young leader on your team might admire you so much that he or she can't imagine you struggling. Honesty and openness are the seeds for authentic connection.

The need to ask powerful questions aligns with the large-sales model I was taught, called SPIN selling[1], a sales methodology practiced at Xerox that was developed by Huthwaite. At the core, SPIN is about asking great questions: from Situation questions, to Problem questions, to Implication questions, to Need-payoff questions.

In theory, it looks easy. Just ask great questions. Of course, there are countless models and methodologies in today's marketing world. Some are better suited for transactional sales, while others are more effective in the complex, solutions-oriented, business-to-business sales world. Regardless of what type of sale or management process you're working with, powerful questions are at the core.

When I look at my personal library of books on both leadership and selling, most of the books contain at least one chapter about the importance of asking questions. Why? For most of us, telling our story is easier than asking powerful questions of someone else. It's often more exciting to talk about a product or service's new bells and whistles than to ask questions to determine if there's any business benefit connected to them.

How did you learn the value of asking great questions? What are some of your school-of-hard-knocks stories that could be the basis for some great questions with your next-gen leader?

Millennials and Powerful Questions

Have you noticed that millennials aren't afraid to ask questions? On the plus side, this is seen as an eagerness to learn and better understand the headwinds they're up against. On the down side, the copious questions have contributed to millennials being thought of as disrespectful or not driven to seek understanding on their own. In my observations, millennials have the ability to ask questions but generally do not ask deeply insightful questions. Those take more practice.

A WORD FROM A MILLENNIAL ...

"Oftentimes I feel as though I'm offending the more experienced person I'm working with by asking questions. In reality, I'm trying to understand why she made a different choice than I would have. I want to understand, not belittle her decision."

As children, we baby boomers asked a lot of questions too. We'd start with Mom or Dad. If they didn't know the answer, then we'd turn to the nearest set of encyclopedias. Today, millennials can instantly get the answer to any question from whatever device is nearest to them.

Access to the Internet from anywhere and at any time has changed all of our lives. But what's unique about millennials is that they've never known any different. They've grown up in a culture where it's acceptable to question an adult's order or instruction. They think it's okay to want an explanation for why something must be done in a certain way. The ease with which they get answers from technology has given them a certain boldness.

A WORD FROM A MILLENNIAL ...

"And with everything on the Internet, we can usually find at least one person who would support our position, further inflating our big heads!"

Your Next-Gen Leader and Powerful Questions

Asking the right questions at the right time is key in business, and this is where you can use your experience to mentor your next-gen leader. When you model a questioning and learning stance for them, you supply tools that will benefit them in all of their relationships and their career.

Following are three instances when you can model tough conversational challenges with powerful questioning skills. When a piece of communication leaves your young leader in the dark, these simple questions should help them gain clarity about what the other person is thinking and feeling.

Conversation Challenge #1

When there's a vague response with little or no detail, keep exploring and digging deeper.

- Can you tell me more? Can you clarify?

- Help me understand ...
- What did you mean when you said _____?

Conversation Challenge #2

When there's confusion about what is being asked or said, and you need clarification so you are responding to the correct issue, ask one of the following questions:

- What an interesting question. Why do you ask?
- I think you're asking _____. Is that correct?
- I'm curious. What's driving you to want to know more about that?

Conversation Challenge #3

When more than a yes or no is needed, ask open-ended questions to trigger further thought. These questions begin with words such as *what* and *how*. For example:

- "What are your thoughts regarding _____?"
- "What do you see as the relationship between _____ and _____?"
- "How do you see this impacting your moving forward?"
- "How does this relate to what you mentioned previously?"

I learned about closed-ended and open-ended questions my first year in sales. They're easy to spot on paper but more difficult to practice. Modeling and working with your next-gen leader on these practical skills will give them a communication leg up as they progress in their leadership roles and responsibilities.

Conversation Challenge #4

When your next-gen leader wants to measure how effective their conversation was, suggest that they think back on the amount of time they spent talking. Compare that to how much time the other person spent talking. Ask them to record these two numbers.

- Percentage of time I talked: _____
- Percentage of time the other person talked: _____

I find that we often spend 80 percent of the time promoting *our* point of view and only 20 percent listening to what the other person has to say. What might happen if we listen for 80 percent of the time instead? Research shows that we're perceived as the following when the prospect/client talks 80 percent of the time:

- More professional
- More knowledgeable
- More competent
- More trustworthy
- Smarter

So, if your next-gen leader wants to raise their IQ, they can start listening more.

Mentor your next-gen leader to practice the power of thoughtful questions. Their doing so will bring meaning to their daily interactions, and their leadership skill set will skyrocket. Let's all continue the journey of becoming better listeners, not just great talkers.

LEADERSHIP LESSON

Ask insightful questions to get meaningful
answers that get to the heart of the issue.
That's when forward momentum happens.

25

Listen Deeply
to Other People

While traveling western North Dakota in my early Xerox days (and logging forty thousand miles a year on my car), I listened to entire volumes of Zig Ziglar books. One of the principles that run like a golden thread through all of Zig's books, articles, and talks is the importance of showing others that we really care about them. I embraced this principle and decided to show my next client how much I care by asking him a great deal of questions about his business.

One morning I walked confidently into a prospect meeting. I'd mapped out excellent questions on my pre-call worksheet. The conversation started out well, but then I saw it had begun to fizzle. I doubled down by asking even more questions. I tried as hard as I could, so I was shocked when I was asked to leave—immediately.

I was escorted out of my prospect's business. Me? Escorted off their premises? I felt devastated and deeply embarrassed. Plus, I was certain I would get fired. I drove back to the office, sobbing uncontrollably in the car and all the way into my manager's office.

Through my sobs, my manager deciphered what had happened. Then he empathetically helped me debrief my failed sales call. He praised my determination to master the questions. However, he pointed out that I had focused too much on the questions and not enough on listening to the answers. Like any great sales manager, he ended the coaching conversation by sending me back out into the field. "You can do it, Danita. You know we only hire the best."

I had wondered, *How do I show prospects and clients that I care about them?* I realized, along with Zig, that I can show I care by asking great questions—and then actually listening to my prospects' and clients' replies.

Have you, like me, learned the hard way the importance of actually listening? Was it at home or at work? That might be a story your next-gen leader would relish and benefit from hearing.

Millennials and Listening

In my work with young leaders, I hear legitimate complaints about how we also fail to listen to them. Here are a few important points they've raised:

- Millennials want to have good relationships with their clients, colleagues, and bosses, but feel this isn't happening. Example: "My boss seems more interested in the numbers I can deliver than he's interested in me."

- Many millennials feel they're unfairly labeled. Example: "Just because I was born in a certain year does not automatically mean I'm lazy and all the other negative things people seem to believe about millennials. I just want my boss to give me a chance and really listen to what I have to say."

- Millennials tell me they become disheartened by the constant negative talk about their generation. Example: "Everybody is talking *about* millennials. And it's all bad. Why don't experienced leaders want to talk *to* us? We would like to hear about their failures, their mistakes, and how they fixed those problems. Then we will listen."

A WORD FROM A MILLENNIAL ...

"That deep need and respect for relationship also drives our every move. This is the reason we are attached to our phones, don't want to work nine-to-five jobs, and are looking for opportunities to become better. If a friend needs us, we want to have the ability to help them right away. When I have an important meeting, or a close friend does, we send each other a message and let them know that we will be offline for two hours. It's out of relationship. We understand there is a time when you need to be in the office at a specific time and there are certain jobs that require those rigid work hours. But many of us are hard workers and we don't like to sit around for hours waiting to leave if we can finish our job in less time."

Listening doesn't come naturally to all of us. Initially, listening deeply to others may feel ... well, scary: "What if I lose my thought? Their perspective might wreck my point of view."; "What happens if I listen to them but they won't listen to me and my perspectives?"; or "They might just be interested in verbally beating me up and telling me how stupid I am."

Listening well requires setting aside our egos and agendas and being vulnerable. It requires courage. The payoff for the courageous listener is abundant. Listening ensures relevance, improves cooperation, deepens relationships, and boosts productivity. And, if you recall from the previous chapter, when a prospect/client talks 80 percent of the time, they perceive us as more professional, more knowledgeable, and more trustworthy.

How to Help Your Next-Gen Leader to Listen Deeply

Listening—deep listening—is critical to reaching the heart of an issue. Only then can the best solutions be discovered.

Here are ways to help your emerging leader develop this critical skill set.

Recognize Listening Derailers

At least half of the sales professionals we assess during our sales audits have listening roadblocks, which has a negative impact on sales performance. Instead of staying zeroed in on listening to the other person, they start thinking about what they're going to say next. They listen to their internal self-talk instead of the other person. Or, if the other person mentions a problem, they begin to think about how they're going to solve the issue. Or, they might have a "brain freeze" and have nothing to say at all.

Whatever happens, the net result is that they stop listening to the other person, losing key information and perspectives that would help deepen understanding and trust. The outcome is that they lose sales. They kill the goose that lays the golden egg. For your promising up-and-comer, this trait is a liability that saps leadership potential.

Walk through your mentee's answers to the following self-test of common beliefs that derail listening:

- "Some people are scary to talk to."
- "I sometimes get tongue-tied when someone asks me a question, especially someone whom I think might criticize me."
- "I have to answer all the questions people ask me."
- "I can't ask too many questions as the other person might get angry with me."
- "I need to avoid people who have treated me rudely or disrespectfully in the past."

About 75 percent of the young people I work with confess to believing one of the above statements. I'm certain your young leader will confess to some of these also. Discuss how these beliefs undermine their ability to build positive relationships.

Then start crafting an action plan that helps them achieve their collaboration goals.

No Multitasking

Your mentee is so adept at multitasking that they may think listening is a multitasking project. I don't know about you, but I've had to learn the hard way that leadership is not a multitasking activity.

When you're talking with your young mentee, make it a rule that neither of you will multitask—no e-mailing and no checking notifications or messages on phones. Turn off the sound of both phones. Close your computer screens so you aren't tempted to glance at them.

A WORD FROM A MILLENNIAL …

"When millennials feel listened to and respected, they will flourish in the workplace."

Don't Get Hijacked

When there's conflict or a difficult topic on the table, listening becomes harder, especially when emotions spark. Then it's easy for our feelings and our agenda to get hijacked, and we end up somewhere completely different from where we anticipated.

The twisting knot in the stomach, the pounding heart, the shortness of breath, and the cold, clammy hands—we've all felt them. As leaders, we've developed strategies for how to handle our stress.

Help your leader develop their own strategies for gaining emotional control so they can stay in the moment and keep listening. Remind your emerging leader of the following:

- Don't take things personally. This outburst is more about the other person who is emotionally upset than it is about you.

- Respond with a clarification question, then keep listening to gain insight into what the other person is thinking and feeling.
- Take notes about what is discussed and concentrate on what is being said. The notes can be used afterward to draw up action plans.
- Break the flow by excusing yourself to get a drink of water or a cup of coffee. Or, change your physical location.
- Take a break if needed. I've adopted the mantra, "Walking *is* working." When I'm really stressed about a situation, I go for a walk. I always come back refreshed with a new perspective.

We all desire to be heard and understood. You can inspire your young leader to advance your business growth, as well as your succession strategies, by showing them how to deeply listen to others. Listening is the tailwind that gets them where they want to go.

A WORD FROM A MILLENNIAL ...

"I fear that some older leaders I know might not take this chapter seriously. The importance of listening in a relationship is right on. Of course, they want their business or company to succeed, but from what I've experienced, older generations really aren't taking us seriously."

LEADERSHIP LESSON

When talking to someone, put down
the technology and listen intently.

26

Dealing with Difficult Conversations

My seventy-something parents observed there was a lack of mentoring for the twenty-somethings who attended their church. So, every other Saturday evening, my parents invite these young people to great home-cooked dinners at The Triple T Ranch. Each informal dinner is followed by an intentional discussion on a leadership topic.

My husband and I attended one of these evenings and had a wonderful, relaxing time around the dinner table. Everyone seemed to truly enjoy hanging out together. When it was time to move into the living room for the more formal discussion, it became silent. No one talked. Thankfully, my parents are great facilitators and listeners and started asking the young leaders open-ended questions. The young people eventually opened up and talked in that fairly intimate, safe setting, and one young person confessed, "I'm petrified to speak in a group, even one this small."

This experience got me thinking. If it was that difficult for them to speak in such a safe environment, how would they fare when they have to deal with conflict and difficult conversations in the workplace?

Millennials might be on the receiving end of a difficult conversation at work. But on other occasions, they'll need to initiate the conversation. I've asked millennials that I mentor what they regard as topics for essential conversations in their careers. Here are a few examples of their responses:

- Wanting a raise or a promotion and not knowing how to bring it up
- Not agreeing with their immediate superior about a serious matter
- Not feeling appreciated or respected by older coworkers
- Rejection of an idea they brought to the table

They've also confided that even when they stir up the courage to have the conversation, they often leave feeling like they weren't heard, and their problem remains unsolved. It felt like a lose-lose to them. They lost because they weren't heard, and an even greater consequence was that they'll be reluctant to bring up other concerns in the future. Clearly this isn't a healthy situation for any business.

A WORD FROM A MILLENNIAL ...

"Take the time to check in often and actually listen and give a response during that conversation. The feedback can be positive or negative, but we need it soon after a discussion. We cannot wait six months for feedback."

Show Your Next-Gen Leader How to Deal with Difficult Conversations

Talking face-to-face about serious matters pushes most of us out of our comfort zones. The way in which you conduct difficult conversations with your next-gen leader will give them insight and experience for each time they'll have to initiate similar conversations.

Following are mentoring tips for how to deal with difficult conversations, maintain strong working relationships, and make the conversations meaningful, less stressful, and more productive.

Take Action Today—Don't Delay

Invite your young leader to have an informal conversation about a topic of concern with a superior as soon as possible. By doing this, the more difficult conversation might be avoided completely. Delaying a conversation or trying to ignore the problem will inevitably escalate the issue.

Explore at Least Three Solutions

Help your next-gen leader to not just identify problems but also be a solution provider. Explore with them at least three possible answers and outcomes. These ideas can be a catalyst for providing even better results than anticipated.

- Educators tell me that one of the trends they observe is that this age group is much more confident when they articulate their argument. However, they often "don't know what they don't know." So, millennials think they get it when they don't really.
- Educators also observe that their students are most apt to dig into their positions instead of sincerely seeking to understand the other person's perspective. So, they are less adept at looking at alternative points of view.

Plan and Prepare

In the book *Crucial Conversations: Tools for Talking When Stakes Are High*, the authors point out the importance of preparation. They suggest asking questions to help oneself plan and prepare, like these:

- "What do I want for me?"
- "What do I want for my superior?"
- "What do I want for our work relationship?"

These questions will help them to be clear about the message they want to deliver, and will help determine a shared goal. Then they can move on to questions about the facts, possible resolutions, and the other party's reaction.

A WORD FROM A MILLENNIAL ...

"While in my new job, I've seen how much this affects the older leaders trying to interact with and coach their upcoming leaders. Plus, I see how important it is for me (and my millennial peers) to be able to adjust to our leaders."

Role Play with a Trusted Outsider

When your young leader feels anxious or stressed about an issue, it will be even more difficult for them to effectively deal with a difficult conversation. Suggest that they act out the conversation with an outsider (someone outside the company) they can trust. This can be their partner, spouse, or close friend. This exercise will help them to be prepared and less nervous when they have the actual discussion. They might also gain new insights into the situation, which can change their perspective about how they view the problem.

A WORD FROM A MILLENNIAL ...

"My friends and I have encountered this weird phenomenon as we enter the workplace. Many of the people in charge are around the same age as our parents. So our bosses tend to take on the role of parent, at least that's how it feels to us. All of the complexities that we have in regard to that relationship end up being reflected in our work performance. Certain aspects of wanting approval, fear of disappointment, anger, or misunderstood expectations are the most common. It can be difficult to see an employer for who they are, which is why the relationship is so important."

Play a Game

Playing games together helps people connect in a different way. Colleagues who don't get along may see a new side of the other person. As a result, stronger relationship bonds can be forged. This leads to better workplace morale.

We're all uniquely wired and have distinct perspectives. Therefore, we have different opinions about difficult topics. Strong emotions are often a part of these conversations, especially when the stakes are high for everyone.

When your next-gen leader is able to receive feedback and effectively communicate their thoughts and feelings, whether they consider the environment safe or not, you'll have accomplished a rewarding task. As they grow in their understanding of their unique strengths, along with valuing the perspectives of others, they'll fuel communication and collaboration so that teamwork is maximized and the team gets where they need to go.

LEADERSHIP LESSON

Dealing effectively with difficult conversations fuels communication and teamwork.

Dear Reader,

We face big problems in our businesses, our families, and our world. We'll only thrive with leaders who respect every person they encounter, regardless of their religion, race, sexual orientation, and political views. With respect as a foundation, we want to understand the other person. This drives our curiosity and the insightfulness of our questions, as well as our deep listening skills. These attributes become even more critical when there is a heated topic, so be sure to practice while it's easy.

We have the substantial responsibility to model respect for our next-gen leaders. Where else will they learn it? Not on social media. We get to guide future leaders to honor and respect themselves and every person they interact with, whether they agree with that person or not.

One of the more difficult conversations for many of us to have with millennials is about spiritual matters, especially with the rise of those who don't identify with any religious group. David Stark's *Reaching Millennials: Proven Methods for Engaging a Younger Generation* is a must-read for those searching for a better way to have a conversation about spiritual matters in the context of a trusted, two-way mentoring relationship.

When I'm hiking the bluffs of western North Dakota and I see geese flying in formation overhead, I think that if the geese can get it, then we can also.

Love never gives up.
Love cares more for others than for self.
Love doesn't want what it doesn't have.
Love doesn't strut,
Doesn't have a swelled head,
Doesn't force itself on others,
Isn't always "me first,"
Doesn't fly off the handle,

Doesn't keep score of the sins of others,
Doesn't revel when others grovel,
Takes pleasure in the flowering of truth,
Puts up with anything,
Trusts God always,
Always looks for the best,
Never looks back,
But keeps going to the end.
1 CORINTHIANS 13:4–7

—Danita

Interview with Jeff Roman, Sr. Director of Marketing & Public Relations of Convoy of Hope

I am embarrassed to admit that I am a bit jaded and skeptical of many nonprofits. However, Convoy of Hope, with a driving passion to feed the world, stands out as a shining star. Charity Navigator awarded them the prestigious Four Star Charity Award. The founders, with North Dakota roots, are thriving today because of the radical kindness of neighbors who helped them in their darkest moment. This kindness fuels their innovative commitment to help those in need both nationally as well as around the world. To be effective, they, like the rest of us, need to be constantly innovating. The feedONE initiative, spearheaded by Jeff Roman, is one of those efforts.

Q: Tell us about Convey of Hope and the feedONE initiative, Jeff.

Jeff: Convoy of Hope is a faith-based nonprofit humanitarian organization. Since 1994, we've been able to serve nearly 80 million people throughout the world by sharing food, water, emergency supplies, agricultural know-how, and opportunities that empower people's lives by freeing them from poverty, disease, and hunger. FeedONE is our campaign to fight hunger. We often collaborate with businesses to raise financial resources and allow their employees, customers, vendors, and friends to partner with us in creative ways to fund our children's feeding initiative. When we provide a hungry child with food, we unlock the door to clean water, education, and hope.

Q: Most millennials want to be involved in a business that is serving a greater cause. What's been your experience in talking with business owners about creating a culture of giving back?

Jeff: I feel that there are two schools of thought right now when it concerns businesses looking for a way to give back and build a culture that fits with the millennial mind-set. Corporate Social Responsibility, or CSR, refers to business practices that involve some type of initiative that is ultimately going to benefit society. Companies of all sizes have taken it upon themselves to start a CSR initiative or have sought ways to take portions of their company's proceeds and give them away to charities.

The second school of thought is about social enterprises. The most classic example of social enterprise is the idea of TOMS Shoes and their "Buy One, Give One" business model. It's the idea that the profits of business are to tackle social problems, improve communities, improve people's life chances, or improve the environment. The difference between CSR and social enterprise is that with social enterprises, the output revolves around social causes, not just the profits. Social enterprise is not only to make profit for the owners and founders, but also to have a substantial impact in the world around them.

Q: Since this is an important cultural dimension for business leaders to be paying attention to in their talent attraction and retention strategies, what are your greatest insights?

Jeff: The number one thing business leaders want is a customizable solution to bring to their employees. Their employees need to feel that they are part of the solution and conversation. That partnership opportunity is key. When we launched feedONE four years ago, we had to be very nimble, and we also had to be ready to create customized solutions for people to engage with us. Business leaders want programs that can be crafted by their own employees.

Q: So, based on your experience, Jeff, what would be some recommendations you would give a business owner who's starting to think about how to create a culture of giving back?

Jeff: I think a lot of business leaders today are very quick to discount the impact of millennials. I think the generation as a whole is fighting a stigma. We hear it come up time and time again. They are lazy and entitled. These are the buzz words that surround their generation, which I think are pretty unfair labels. It's time to drop the labels and realize that this generation represents one of the deepest wells of potential that we have ever seen.

Q: How might these stereotypes affect businesses?

Jeff: Stereotypes cause business leaders to become very short-sighted. They don't realize that, eventually, millennials are going to be the bulk of their consumers and employees. They need to first and foremost understand that they're dealing with a generation whose hearts and minds function differently. The priorities that they hold as important are more traditional values such as time, relationships, and impact on the community. If business leaders take an approach to understand how they're communicating to this generation, then they can begin to create a culture that will make sense.

Q: Can you give us an example?

Jeff: Successful business leaders work with the millennial generation to find ways to support volunteerism. It's about flexibility. It could be paid time off specifically for volunteer work, or time to be able to go on a mission trip, or time to volunteer at a local food bank during normal working hours. Tackling that idea of time and having an open mind would just be one functional example of how business leaders can begin to create a culture of support for the desires of the millennial generation.

I think business leaders need to realize the impact they have on the world around them. It's easy to recognize that they have an incredible legacy to leave their family, their employees, and other leaders in the community.

That impact can happen when they make a choice to engage with an organization like feedONE and Convoy of Hope or other organizations. It doesn't take a lot to make a big difference. In our case of feedONE, it's just one example of how a ten-dollar gift, less than the price of a typical business lunch, will feed a child for an entire month. When business leaders realize that their legacy reaches farther than they ever imagined, they will truly change the world.

Q: Share with us the quote from the home page of feedONE .com. It's powerful.

Jeff: Mother Teresa once said, "If you can't feed a hundred, then just feed one." We've taken her words to heart and believe that if this generation is unleashed to solve the planet's great challenges, it will produce a whole new world.

Every person must decide whether he will walk in the light of creative altruism or in the darkness of destructive selfishness. Life's most persistent and urgent question is, "What are you doing for others?"

—Martin Luther King

Part 2

Inspire the
Investment Effect

Definition: An outward focus that leverages
my strengths to empower others so that
we live with purpose and meaning.

27

The Investment Effect and Leadership

A few years ago, I was involved with a team that was establishing a new model of economic development in Tanzania. The primary goal of our trip was to inspect a new model of economic improvement for developing nations. One of the projects involved rethinking the entire value chain, from crop to cash. This process would empower farmers instead of making them dependent on foreign charity.

After landing in one of the largest and busiest African cities, Dar es Salaam, we traveled for hours on a hot, overcrowded bus to Iringa, in central Tanzania. From Iringa we drove six hours over a rugged trail that had been partly washed out by the rainy season. Finally, we reached our destination—a tiny village deep in the mountainous interior part of Tanzania.

Rebecca, a widow who was raising two teenage boys and caring for her elderly parents, joined ten male village elders to greet us. She was included in the reception party because she was respected as a budding entrepreneur. This woman, who was under five feet tall, welcomed me with a great smile and a warm hug, and called me her sister. I loved the people's enthusiasm, and I instantly loved Rebecca.

As we talked, she shared her dream. It was one that seemed impossible to achieve, considering that widows in Tanzania are at the bottom of the social structure.

My husband, Gordon, taught the entire village about modern farming practices that would save them from days and months of backbreaking labor. With each new tip, the women danced and gave a Tanzanian cheer. Rebecca, an eager learner, soaked it all in. She began to catch a vision of how an investment of her time, talent, and resources could serve others.

By the end of day three, I had the utmost respect for Rebecca. She was committed to helping not only her own family but the village to become more prosperous. I thought, *What can I do? How can I inspire the investment effect in this tiny village?* My opportunity arrived on a Saturday morning. The village elders invited me to preach at their church on Sunday and said Rebecca would be my interpreter. I felt deeply honored.

Because I'd been attending seminary in the States, I knew the first steps in sermon preparation. I diligently did all my exegetical and hermeneutical work on the text I would use from the apostle Paul: "Now to Him who is able to do exceedingly abundantly above all that we ask or think, according to the power that works in us" (Ephesians 3:20 NKJV).

However, the more I dug into the ancient text, the more I realized I was wrestling with cultural differences. This was Africa, not America. I grew nervous. I wanted to teach a truth that transcends time, space, and cultures. This principle applied not just in the Westernized, industrialized world, but it was also core for this African culture. Finally, I thought I had it nailed down.

Rebecca stopped by my hostel at about five in the afternoon for rehearsal. My goal was to outline everything for her so she could interpret correctly. We sat down on the hostel's front porch, and I painstakingly explained my three-point sermon to her. When I finished, she was quiet for a bit, reflecting. Then she said, "So what you're saying is this: God, the Great Entrepreneur, made us in his image. We are entrepreneurs at our core, therefore we can be creative and innovative in how we do our work and live our lives, so that we can serve others. As we use our heads, hearts, and hands to work through the tasks before us, we can envision and implement new ways of raising our potatoes as a cash crop. Is that correct?"

I was stunned. Rebecca immediately got it. The next day she

eloquently translated the sermon into a charge that everyone in her village understood—head, heart, and hands. It was a charge to develop an invest effect.

A WORD FROM A MILLENNIAL ...

> "I feel like the idea of emulating God's example will resonate with some millennials. Some millennials would like to feel as though their natural entrepreneurial skills are a talent planted in them by a higher power/God and that they have a responsibility to develop those skills and talents fully, instead of trying to be like God."

An Outward Focus Leverages the Gifts and Talents of Everyone

A leader like Rebecca knew that, in order to bring her dream fully to life, there had to be action—a series of small steps that would move her and the community forward. She knew they all had a better chance of achieving their goals if they worked together as a team.

As I reflect on Rebecca's mind-set, I realize she had other options. One option would be to use her gifts and talents while focusing inward, only on her own goals and objectives, not the needs of her entire village. Then she would be the "everything's about me" leader, but she would include others when it advanced her own agenda or made her look good.

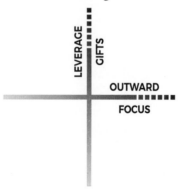

Rebecca also had the option to be focused outward, but without utilizing her gifts, talents, and resources. Leaders like this have good intentions but lack traction. They talk, talk, talk, but rarely do. If they do manage to get to the "do" part, they often spin their wheels because they aren't leveraging the talents and resources of the team. These leaders struggle to inspire teams to work toward their common goals and hardly ever make a tangible difference in tackling their visions.

Millennials and the Investment Effect

Even as you proactively and intentionally invest in your next-gen leader, the end goal is to inspire them to invest in others, to make a positive difference in a way that only they are wired to do. This serving attitude is imperative for meaningful, lasting impact. Your insight, discernment, and wisdom, in combination with their passion and vision, create a relationship that fuels well-grounded leadership.

Each of us must use our wisdom and life experiences to show next-gen leaders that they also have enormous wealth to share—wealth that goes beyond monetary value.

A WORD FROM A MILLENNIAL ...

"I have seen how we are very socially minded, especially as a group, compared to gen Xers who are currently running most of the world in general."

LEADERSHIP LESSON

Consider how to serve every
person you meet today.

※ **28**

Share
Your Wealth

When I prepared for our Tanzanian trip, I had many concerns. How do I not be a stereotypical, ethnocentric Westerner? How do I respect and honor their culture, while calling them into a brighter future? I knew that I was steeped in America's definition of wealth: financial independence.

Aware of my struggle, a friend dared me to broaden my definition. He suggested that wealth, and thus poverty, come in many forms: physical, intellectual, relational, spiritual, and financial. It sounded like a reasonable model, so I vowed to keep this perspective.

As we immersed ourselves in the Tanzanian culture, these various concepts of wealth became more alive to me. Yes, I had financial wealth, especially compared to the subsistence farmers we met on the trip. In Rebecca, I began to see the profound spiritual wealth—not based on going to seminary, but based on her deep, practical, rubber-meets-the-road relationship with the Creator.

Rebecca also demonstrated relational wealth. She invited us to meet her parents and two young sons as if we were family. With a happy smile, she showed us around her two-room clay-baked brick home and explained that the constant fire, just outside the door, was for cooking meals, telling stories at night, and showing hospitality to neighbors and villagers who needed assistance.

Rebecca modeled that investing these kinds of wealth in others is a win-win—they can bring meaning to the lives of others while fueling their desire to live with purpose and meaning. Her example summoned me to be a wise steward of all the kinds of wealth I had.

A WORD FROM A MILLENNIAL ...

"From what I have come across, millennials care less about financial gain as compared to gen Xers and baby boomers. They grew up in a system with abundant opportunity to grow financially. Hard work = major financial gains. Most millennials came of age in a post 9/11 world, a global financial crisis, and two wars. I have friends who have never moved out of their childhood home because their parents still enjoy providing for them. They would rather work random jobs that bring them happiness, flexibility, and the means to travel. In some cases they cannot leave home because their salary cannot cover both rent/mortgage and student loan repayments. With lack of opportunity to advance steadily in the workforce, we look for satisfaction in other places, such as social causes and personal fulfillment."

Millennials and Sharing Their Wealth

Most of the recent studies and surveys on millennials reveal that this generation loves sharing their gifts and skills. If you recall from earlier in the book, a Pew Research Center study found that 84 percent believe that making a difference in the world is more important than professional recognition. Also, 92 percent believe that business success should be measured by more than just profit.[1]

Millennials are at the forefront of using social media to participate in various causes, not only in their own communities but around the globe. This global awareness affects their reactions to situations closer to home.

How do we inspire millennials to take inventory of all their forms of wealth and invest them to help and empower others? In doing so, their lives can brim with purpose and meaning.

Your Next-Gen Leader and Sharing Their Wealth

The hunger to be involved in making a difference for others, to be world changers, is a key driver for millennials. How do we tap into this great character quality and inspire millennials to share their wealth, whether it is relational, physical, intellectual, spiritual, or financial?

What kind of difference does your next-gen leader want to make? What are the causes and issues that are important to them?

A WORD FROM A MILLENNIAL ...

"A good boss will know the causes that are important to their employees, especially with younger people. We care about work-life balance, the social position of the company, being transparent about investments, and sustainability. The concept of 'work life' and 'home life' almost do not exist anymore as we strive to have a purpose behind everything we do. Many of us were raised with the philanthropic philosophy that our job is to earn lots of money so we can donate it to a charity doing good work. We have also noticed that our kind intentions have created a culture of dependency, not empowerment. So we've begun shifting models to micro-financing and other strategies to teach people to fish on their own."

The following ideas may help you spark a dialogue with your mentee on sharing all forms of their wealth with others. Remember, this is a two-way discussion. You'll want to share your own responses to the statements. It may be helpful to reveal aspects of your journey, discussing how each of these statements might have been answered differently, depending on your season of life. Your openness will provide long-term inspiration as your mentee navigates their own seasons of life.

Explore Your Wealth

Complete these sentences together with your next-gen leader:

- I think my best gifts that I can share with others are ____.
- Today I served others by using my gifts when I ____.
- I want my talents to be recognized by/through ____.

Then consider this question with them: Where might I find opportunities to align my gifts and talents with my calling in life?

Broaden Your Wealth

Broaden their perspective by asking them, "Where and how might you share your wealth today at work? At home?"

- Relational wealth?
- Physical wealth (time and/or physical labor)?
- Intellectual or creative wealth?
- Spiritual wealth?
- Financial wealth?

Grow Your Wealth

Rebecca was committed to growing potatoes. As a child on The Triple T Ranch, I would walk by fields of wheat and be reminded of the words of Jesus: "Listen carefully: Unless a grain of wheat is buried in the ground, dead to the world, it is never any more than a grain of wheat. But if it is buried, it sprouts and reproduces itself many times over. In the same way, anyone who holds on to life just as it is destroys that life. But if you let it go, reckless in your love, you'll have it forever, real and eternal" (John 12:24–25). I'm reminded that in order to grow our wealth, we usually have to be willing to sacrifice and give up a certain way of thinking or doing things. Talk with your mentee about how this concept might apply to them as they seek to make the impact they envision.

A WORD FROM A MILLENNIAL ...

"I don't know about this. Most people in their twenties and early thirties have already understood through their own experiences to value things outside of financial gain. I think that some millennials would appreciate an older boss/mentor to value these things as well and lead by example. Some ideas would be to have the company sponsor a company-wide Big Brother/Big Sister initiative that takes place during work hours, have a community garden at the office where people can sign up to tend to it and benefit from the crop yield, give financial bonuses to people who document ten hours of community service per quarter, or maintain a 'hobby fund' for employees and provide both time and financial matching. These are ways to build millennials to be more well-rounded."

I confess that I need my own paradigm of giving and philanthropy to be revisited. I had recently attended a string of fundraising events, all for incredible nonprofits doing great work around the world. My heartstrings had been tugged—and were getting weary of getting tugged. That's when I read North Dakota governor Doug Burgum's insights, which I believe are important for emerging leaders and entrepreneurs to consider. Doug is an entrepreneur who sold Great Plains to Microsoft, where he then served as senior vice president. He said, "I've been involved in making payroll every two weeks for the last thirty-three years. I've created a lot of jobs over that time personally. I've also had the chance in the later part of my life to be involved in philanthropy. And I understand that the best philanthropy contribution people can make is creating jobs. That's the gift that keeps on giving. That's the contribution that gives to the entire community."[2]

LEADERSHIP LESSON

Take inventory of all your forms of wealth—relational, physical, intellectual, spiritual, and financial— then invest them in others.

29

Find the Strengths
in Others

Many years after taking the StrengthsFinder survey, I took the inventory again. Thirty-four talents are identified in this survey, and most people have three that stand out as particularly strong. For me, Maximizer, Achiever, and Activator rise to the top the list.

When our talents are used to serve others, they become strengths that benefit everyone. However, if not stewarded wisely and productively from strong character cores, our talents can be a detriment to ourselves and those around us. I'm certain we can all think of someone in our life who is very talented but uses their gifts for destructive, self-serving purposes.

Millennials and Finding Strengths

By now, we're all familiar with the list of negative millennial attributes: lazy, ungrateful, entitled, and narcissistic. Do you also ask, "What on earth will become of this generation?" I can assure you that every generation has said something similar about the younger generation.

When I talk with millennials, I hear a different perspective. I was inspired and excited when I read some of the replies I received from millennials on this question: "What do you regard to be your generation's biggest strength?" Following are several thoughtful responses:

- "We are inventive. There are more people on earth now than ever before, which means a person has to outwork others and get creative in order to compete for available jobs and achieve success. Novelty is easier with the Internet, and we are able to reach large audiences. We can use many forms of media that never existed before."

- "We embrace change. We grew up in an environment where things change frequently, especially in our communication channels due to the invention of various social media platforms. Baby boomers may call that fickle, but I would say we aren't as afraid of the pain of change. If something better comes up, of course we'll move that way. This trait is key for improving a business. I see the unwillingness to change all the time with companies, and I'm disgusted with it. I actually get annoyed when a person or a company doesn't adapt a better system or technology as quickly as they should. Any company that doesn't adapt incrementally will be surpassed by companies that are run by millennials."

- "We are creative. Every day there is something new in the world that a millennial has accomplished or created. And that's a real feat at this point in history!"

- "We are an information-seeking generation. We believe that it's better to be informed than to be blissfully ignorant of important issues."

- "We adapt and evolve with the situations and challenges that are put in front of us, and we want to get in front of as many situations/challenges as we can. I feel the older generation tends to play situations safer. This could be because of where they are in their careers, but I've noticed they often take their time making decisions about, and responding to, challenges."

- "We are versatile. For those of us toward the end of the millennial age spectrum, we grew up in a span of time when we had exposure to both technology-light and technology-driven processes. For example, as elementary students we were the first age group to learn both cursive and typing in school. We also learned how to do reports with both physical and online encyclopedias. With exposure to both sides, I believe while we thrive on the fast pace of our technology-driven world, we also have respect for the drastic changes that have taken place for the generations that have come before us."

- "We are entrepreneurial. Almost half of my friends said they would rather launch their own business ventures than be in jobs they didn't enjoy. And they're willing to sacrifice to make it happen. They'll sacrifice short-term things, such as lifestyle, saving and spending habits, and even relationships, for long-term success."

These replies all point to one predominant takeaway: Millennials, at least some of them, aren't frazzled by hurdles that we, the experienced generation, see as significant stumbling blocks. They view all of the above traits as positives that can make them sought-after, valuable assets to any business.

Your Next-Gen Leader and Finding Strengths in Others

What strengths does your next-gen leader think they have? What do you see? Based on your leadership experience, how might you build on and leverage these strengths in pursuing their passions and goals? How might those passions be aligned with the work they're doing currently?

Suggest the following three steps to your next-gen mentee so you help them identify their own strengths as well as the strengths in others.

Collaborate with People Who Make You Stronger

Our strengths might easily become our weaknesses if we don't value the various gifts and talents of our colleagues. For example, some people will stall out on every single project if they don't work with teammates who have detail-oriented talent. That's where a survey tool, like StrengthsFinder or DiSC, can be insightful. Such tools can help us discover more about ourselves, both strengths and areas in need of growth, plus they open our eyes to see the strengths and vulnerabilities of our colleagues. Once we know this info, we can effectively work together and support each other.

Focus on Finding Strengths

Everyone has gifts and talents. Look for them. Be intentional in identifying them. Then make a habit of affirming the strengths you see in others. Imagine how relationships can improve when you communicate positively with people who are struggling to find their way in new situations and environments. Everyone has proficiencies. Affirming their strengths at optimal times will inspire them to believe they have the capability to be strong contributors to their teams.

Give the Gift of Gratefulness

When conflicts arise, finding strengths to acknowledge in others can be difficult. However, foster your next-gen leader's ability to find and acknowledge them anyway. Have them think of at least three things that they are grateful for in a given person or situation. It may take a few extra minutes or even a couple of hours to come up with three positives. Do it anyway. Then, be grateful for those positives. There's a growing body of research on the benefits of being grateful. Gratefulness is a gift you give yourself that empowers others, leverages all your talents, and provides deep meaning and purpose to life.

As an experienced business leader, set the example for your next-gen leader as they begin a lifelong habit of finding strengths in themselves and others, as well as resisting both overconfidence and feelings of intimidation. It's combined strengths that make a team great.

I was reminded of the power of gratefulness when I read this devotional, written by Rick Warren: "Thank God in all things. When you pray, pray with thanksgiving. The healthiest human emotion is not love but gratitude. It actually increases your immunities. It makes you more resistant to stress and less susceptible to illness. People who are grateful are happy. But people who are ungrateful are miserable because nothing makes them happy. They're never satisfied. It's never good enough. So if you cultivate the attitude of gratitude, of being thankful in everything, it reduces stress in your life."[1]

Work with your next-gen leader to leverage their talents to serve others. In so doing, their talent becomes a strength that benefits those around them and serves a greater purpose.

LEADERSHIP LESSON

Find the strengths in others. It creates
positive energy and builds momentum.

30

Love Is the
Ultimate Measure

"We haven't talked enough about *love*."

I had just finished teaching a two-hour session on Sales for Emerging Entrepreneurs. Budding tech entrepreneurs in the audience were paired with mentors and investors with the hope of accelerating their business growth. As I wrapped up the training, the company's CEO, a respected entrepreneur and investor, interjected, "Danita, this has been great, but there's one thing we haven't spent enough time on today."

You know how a dozen thoughts can whiz through your head in a matter of seconds? My thoughts went something like this: *I'm pretty thorough. What could I have missed? I've been relentless in stressing how critical it is to deeply understand our prospects' frustrations and headaches, as well as their goals, before we start the data dump about all the great "stuff" we've engineered for them. Was he hoping I would talk about technical competence, the sales process, or sales metrics?*

Instead of dumping all those preemptive self-defense points on him, I ask him to expound. "Tell me more."

"You're missing a critical link," he said.

Again, my thoughts raced. But I set them aside to keep listening.

The CEO continued, "We haven't talked enough about *love*. To truly serve our employees, clients, and prospects, we need to love them."

Love. I confess I was thrown off by the word. When I read the ancient Scriptures, I'm often reminded that love is the ultimate measure of my life, but it's not a common topic in the business world. However, this entrepreneurial guru, whose life goal was to inspire emerging entrepreneurs and leaders, actually thought we needed to talk more about love—in a business meeting.

Millennials and Love

Research has shown that the more people feel loved at work, the more engaged and productive they are. According to the 2014 *Harvard Business Review* article "Employees Who Feel Love Perform Better," "Employees who felt they worked in a loving, caring culture reported higher levels of satisfaction and team-work. They showed up to work more often."[1]

While this might be true for every generation, I believe love can have a particularly positive impact on your millennial team members. Numerous studies on millennials report that this so-called self-absorbed generation is passionate about these things:

- Donating money to charity (they will conduct an online search first to find out if the charity is doing what they say they're doing)
- Volunteering
- Making a positive difference in the world

Your Next-Gen Leader and Love

What vision can you give your next-gen leader about how they might leave their own inspiring legacy of great leadership?

The exhortation by Ken Blanchard and Phil Hodges in *Lead Like Jesus* may be a goal to work toward: "A godly leader in the community finds common ground and reconciliation with people of diverse opinions, backgrounds, priorities, and spiritual perspectives. Lovingly, they speak in truth and courage with good will and tolerance without wavering from moral and ethical conviction."[2] Notice the word *lovingly* again.

Then, I think of the greatest commandment from Jesus: "Love the Lord your God with all your heart and with all your soul and with all your strength and with all your mind, and [love] your neighbor as yourself" (Luke 10:27 ESV).

There's the word again, love.

And isn't that what drove my friend Rebecca in Tanzania? Love for her family and for the children who needed food, education, and medical attention?

What might love look like today in the business world? Here are practical ways to inspire your next-gen leader to operationalize this word that we don't often use in a business setting.

- Recognize when someone goes the extra mile. Show love and caring by complimenting a job well done via a handwritten note of appreciation.
- Do your work with excellence. (In fact, this is one of the primary ways in which we can live out the great commandment, to love God and love others.)
- Give a smile. As Mother Teresa said, "We shall never know all the good that a simple smile can do."
- Tell someone you see regularly how they positively impact your day.

Another mentor of mine, the late Zig Ziglar, put it well: "You never know when a moment and a few sincere words can have an impact on a life."[3]

LEADERSHIP LESSON

Love is the ultimate measure of our lives.
Show love in all you do and say.

Dear Reader,

In high school, I announced I was planning to use St. Francis of Assisi's famous prayer as the closing to my graduation speech. Not everyone was impressed.

"St. Francis of Assisi wasn't a rich man, so you can't use him to measure success," the superintendent instructed me. "Danita, your job is to inspire leaders to be successful. St. Francis, he wasn't successful. He was just a poor monk. To inspire leaders to success, you need a stronger image."

In spite of his concern, I believed St. Francis' prayer was apropos. Even though it was written close to a thousand years ago, every word of his prayer still carries a strong moral message for today. Then, as now, the Prayer of St. Francis calls us to a higher purpose—an ideal that each of us can strive for in all aspects of our life, especially as we seek to maximize our businesses, mobilize our leaders and realize our leadership legacy.

To this day, the prayer hangs in my office as a daily reminder to answer the call to servant leadership in my business and personal life. I share it with you in the hope that it will encourage you as you shift gears to coach, mentor, and lead with love the up-and-coming leaders in your sphere of influence. For, indeed, love is the ultimate measure of our lives.

Lord, make me an instrument of your peace:
where there is hatred, let me sow love;
where there is injury, pardon;
where there is doubt, faith;
where there is despair, hope;
where there is darkness, light;
where there is sadness, joy.

O divine Master, grant that I may not so much seek
to be consoled as to console,

to be understood as to understand,
to be loved as to love.
For it is in giving that we receive,
it is in pardoning that we are pardoned,
and it is in dying that we are born to eternal life. Amen.
—SAINT FRANCIS OF ASSISI

"Give, and it will be given to you. A good measure,
pressed down, shaken together and running over, will be
poured into your lap. For with the measure you use, it
will be measured to you."
LUKE 6:38 NIV

—Danita

Appendix 1

The Five Capitals:
Key Concept Overview for the Personal

Jesus wasn't just a simple carpenter. He was a builder. He built the most successful enterprise the world has ever seen. He also knows how to build your life and your business better than you do. If you'll let him, he'll build (through you) a life that's integrated, fruitful, and fulfilling.

Here's an overview of the Five Capitals, based on Matthew 25 and Luke 16:

- Spiritual Capital is based on the relationship we have with God. It's the most valuable of all the capitals. It's measured in wisdom and power.
- Relational Capital is the relational equity (or trust) we've built up (or eroded) with others. It's both the quality and depth of our relationships. It's measured in influence and impact.
- Physical Capital is the time and energy we have available to invest. Time is the great equalizer. We have one life to make the most of. It's measured in hours and minutes.
- Intellectual Capital is the creativity and knowledge we have available to invest. The skills and competences we learn allow us to thrive in life. It's measured in creativity and insight.
- Financial Capital is simply the money-tangible resources we have available to invest. It's about stewarding well all the resources we have. It's measured in dollars and cents.[1]

The Five Capitals:
Key Concept Overview for Business

What's amazing is that the Five Capitals concept works in the business world as well! The best companies, whether they realize it or not, invest in all five capitals and keep them in the right order. Here's the business translation/application

- Spiritual Capital is your Brand Identity—going after something bigger than yourself. It's the combination of your company's vision and values.
- Relational Capital is the Company Culture—it's creating an atmosphere that's both healthy and productive, not busy or toxic. It's the quality and depth of your relationships at work.
- Physical Capital is the Rhythms and Cycles of your industry. Great companies take a marathon (not a sprint) approach to the long-term viability and sustainability of the organization. Continually focusing on new product innovation and current product development.
- Intellectual Capital is the intentional Training and Development of employees within an organization. Great companies hire great talent at the bottom and then develop them up. The skills and competences we learn allow us to thrive in life. It's measured in creativity and insight.
- Financial Capital is about Market Share/Profitability— it's the good stewardship and management of resources tasked to the leaders. Using them for advancement, generosity and good in the world.[2]

Reflection: What's the order of your company's capitals? What might you do to align them in such a way as to make a greater impact?

Appendix 2

Spiritual Pathways:
Excerpt from *Letters from the King*:
A Devotional Parable of Spiritual Discovery

God has crafted each of us uniquely. Therefore, it seems reasonable that we each have a distinctive pattern in how we communicate with him and how we strengthen ourselves mentally, emotionally, and spiritually. On a scale of 1 to 10 (with 10 being "this works well for me"), rate yourself to discover which of the following spiritual pathways or practices (adapted from *God Is Closer Than You Think* by John Ortberg) work well for you.

- Intellectual Pathway (Matthew 22:37). I connect with God through the Intellectual Pathway because I:
    - enjoy in-depth teaching about God and the Bible;
    - study Scripture, using concordances and other resources; and
    - attend lectures by biblical scholars when possible.
    - Rating: _____
- Relationship Pathway (Acts 2:42–47). I feel God's presence best when I'm in a deep relationship with other Christian believers. Some of the ways in which I follow the Relationship Pathway include:
    - attending local church services;
    - being part of a small group; and
    - participating in community experiences.
    - Rating: _____

- Serving Pathway (Matthew 25:45). I choose the Serving Pathway to feel God's presence in my life, because:
  - helping others comes naturally to me;
  - serving others helps me feel fulfilled; and
  - attending to the physical needs of others is energizing.
  - Rating: _____
- Worship Pathway (Psalm 122:1). I choose the Worship Pathway to connect with God, because I enjoy the following:
  - praising and worshiping;
  - praying and singing with others; and
  - giving God glory and honor on a regular basis.
  - Rating: _____
- Activist Pathway (Micah 6:8). I'm passionate to be involved through action, therefore I choose the Activist Pathway. This path suits my spirituality best because I am:
  - energizing with a high level of enthusiasm and energy;
  - stimulated by challenges; and
  - flourishing when I'm involved in causes that lead to transformation and social justice.
  - Rating: _____
- Contemplation Pathway (Isaiah 26:3). I prefer the Contemplation Pathway. God is most present to me when I:
  - remove distractions and have uninterrupted time alone;
  - include images and metaphors to help me pray; and
  - listen to God in silence and solitude.
  - Rating: _____

- Creation Pathway (Psalm 19:1). I follow the Creation Pathway because I feel God's presence through nature. I enjoy:
  - walking in the mountains or at a lakeside for communion with God;
  - church camping and outdoor events;
  - gardening; and
  - riding a motorcycle through the great outdoors.
  - Rating: ____

Notes

Chapter 1

1 "Millennials at work: Reshaping the workplace," *PwC*, 2011, https://www.pwc.com/m1/en/services/consulting/documents/millennials-at-work.pdf.

2 "A Quarter of Millennials Who Live at Home Don't Work—or Study," *Bloomberg*, April 20, 2017, https://www.bloomberg.com/news/articles/2017-04-20/a-quarter-of-millennials-who-live-at-home-don-t-work-or-study.

3 Gordon Tredgold, "29 Surprising Facts That Explain Why Millennials See the World Differently," *Inc.*, May 2, 2016, https://www.inc.com/gordon-tredgold/29-surprising-facts-about-millennials-and-what-motivates-them.html.

4 Tim Elmore, *Artificial Maturity: Helping Kids Meet the Challenge of Becoming Authentic Adults* (San Francisco: Jossey-Bass, 2012), 4.

5 Ken Dychtwald, Tamera J. Erickson, and Bob Morison, "It's Time to Retire Retirement," *Harvard Business Review*, March 2004, https://hbr.org/2004/03/its-time-to-retire-retirement.

Chapter 2

1 "Cowboy Ethics," *Center for Cowboy Ethics and Leadership*, http://cowboyethics.org/cowboy-ethics/.

2 Doug Lennick and Fred Kiel, PhD, *Moral Intelligence: Enhancing Business Performance and Leadership Success* (Upper Saddle River, NJ: Pearson Education, Inc., 2008), xxxv.

3 N. T. Wright, *After You Believe: Why Christian Character Matters* (San Francisco: HarperOne, 2010), as cited in http://www.christianitytoday.com/ct/2017/may/science-of-sinning-less.html?TB_iframe=true&width=370.8&height=658.8&start=7.

Chapter 3

1 http://www.chronicle.com/.

2 Peter Gray, PhD, "Declining Student Resilience: A Serious Problem for Colleagues," *Psychology Today*, September 22, 2015, https://www.psychologytoday.com/blog/freedom-learn/201509/declining-student-resilience-serious-problem-colleges.

3 Nick Shore, "Turning On the No-Collar Workforce," *MediaPost*, March 15, 2012, http://www.mediapost.com/publications/article/170109/turning-on-the-no-collar-workforce.html#axzz2VLtY1afW.

Chapter 4

1 Sheree Johnson, "New Research Sheds Light on Daily Ad Exposures," *SJ Insights*, September 29, 2014, https://sjinsights.net/2014/09/29/new-research-sheds-light -on-daily-ad-exposures/.

Chapter 6

1 "Better Money Habits Millennial Report," *Better Money Habits/Bank of America*, https://bettermoneyhabits.bankofamerica.com/content/dam/bmh/pdf/2014 -millennial-report.pdf.
2 David D. Burns, MD, *Feeling Good: The New Mood Therapy* (New York: Avon Books, 1999), 88.

Chapter 7

1 David Horsager, *The Trust Edge* (New York: Free Press, 2012), 1.
2 Chris Cillizza, "Millennials Don't Trust Anyone. That's a Big Deal," *The Washington Post*, April 30, 2015, https://www.washingtonpost.com/news/the-fix /wp/2015/04/30/millennials-dont-trust-anyone-what-else-is-new/?utm_term =.639c3eeb1fac.
3 Emily Badger, "Who Millennials Trust, and Don't Trust, Is Driving the New Economy," April 16, 2015, *The Washington Post*, https://www.washingtonpost .com/news/wonk/wp/2015/04/16/who-millennials-trust-and-dont-trust-is -driving-the-new-economy/?utm_term=.db7d1cc86490.
4 David H. Maister, David H. Green, and Robert M. Galford, *The Trusted Advisor* (New York: Simon and Schuster Ltd., 2000), 4.

Chapter 8

1 http://www.careerbuilder.com/share/aboutus/pressreleasesdetail.aspx?sd=1/26 /2017&siteid=cbpr&sc_cmp1=cb_pr985_&id=pr985&ed=12/31/2017
2 Patrick Lencioni, *The Advantage* (San Francisco: Jossey-Bass, 2012), 57.

Chapter 10

1 https://shcs.ucdavis.edu/sites/default/files/documents/NCHA-II_SPRING_2015 .pdf.

Chapter 11

1 "Your Brain Has a 'Delete' Button—Here's How to Use It," *Fast Company*, May 11, 2016, https://www.fastcompany.com/3059634/your-brain-has-a-delete -button-heres-how-to-use-it.

Chapter 12

1 Tom Ziglar, "If You Aim at Nothing …" *Ziglar*, June 2, 2016, https://www.ziglar .com/articles/if-you-aim-at-nothing-2/.

Chapter 13

1 "American Psychological Association Survey Shows Money Stress Weighing on Americans' Health Nationwide," *American Psychological Association*, February 4, 2015, http://www.apa.org/news/press/releases/2015/02/money-stress.aspx.

2 Amit Chowdhry, "Research Links Facebook and Social Media Use to Depression," *Forbes*, April 30, 2016, https://www.forbes.com/sites/amitchowdhry /2016/04/30/study-links-heavy-facebook-and-social-media-usage-to-depression /#71593ced4b53.

Chapter 14

1 Brandon Rigoni and Bailey Nelson, "Few Millennials Are Engaged at Work," *Gallup*, August 30, 2016, http://www.gallup.com/businessjournal/195209 /few-millennials-engaged-work.aspx.

2 "How Millennials Want to Work and Live," *Gallup*, http://www.gallup.com/reports /189830/millennials-work-live.aspx?utm_source=gbj&utm_medium=copy&utm _campaign=20160830-gbj.

3 RightNow Media, "Work as Worship," *YouTube*, March 27, 2013, https://www .youtube.com/watch?v=HukWGekxrGU.

Chapter 15

1 Amy Adkins, "What Millennials Want From Work and Life," *Gallup*, May 11, 2016, http://www.gallup.com/businessjournal/191435/millennials-work-life.aspx.

2 Caroline Leaf, *Switch on Your Brain: The Key to Peak Happiness, Thinking and Health* (Grand Rapids: Baker Books, 2013), 63.

Chapter 16

1 "The Deloitte Millennial Survey," *Deloitte*, 2016, https://www2.deloitte.com /content/dam/Deloitte/global/Documents/About-Deloitte/gx-millenial-survey -2016-exec-summary.pdf.

2 Albert E. N. Gray, "The Common Denominator of Success," *Amnesta.net*, http:// www.amnesta.net/mba/thecommondenominatorofsuccess-albertengray.pdf.

3 Bradley Wright, "The Science of Sinning Less," *Christianity Today*, April 21, 2017, 35–41.

Chapter 17

1 "Are You Extrinsically or Intrinsically Motivated?" *Lifescript*, http://www.lifescript .com/quizzes/personality/are_you_extrinsically_or_intrinsically_motivated.aspx.

2 Tom Rath, *StrengthsFinder 2.0* (New York: Gallup Press, 2007), as cited from http://www.goodreads.com/quotes/310979-when-we-re-able-to-put-most-of-our -energy-into.

Chapter 18

1 Marta Velázquez, "The Year of Sisu 2015: An Interview with Emilia Lahti," *Positive Psychology News*, March 2, 2015, http://positivepsychologynews.com/news/marta-velazquez/2015030231101.

Chapter 19

1 Larry Bossidy and Ram Charan, *Execution: The Discipline of Getting Things Done* (New York: Crown Business, 2002), 67.

Chapter 20

1 Warren Berger, "The Secret Phrase Top Innovators Use," *Harvard Business Review*, September 17, 2012, https://hbr.org/2012/09/the-secret-phrase-top-innovato.

Chapter 21

1 Stephen Morris, "Domino Chain Reaction (Short Version)," *YouTube*, October 4, 2009, https://www.youtube.com/watch?v=5JCm5FY-dEY.

Chapter 22

1 Steve Wilkens and Mark L. Sanford, *Hidden Worldviews: Eight Cultural Stories That Shape Our Lives* (Downers Grove, IL: InterVarsity Press, 2009), 13.

Chapter 23

1 "Welcome Remarks to Employees," *U.S. Department of State*, February 2, 2017, https://www.state.gov/secretary/remarks/2017/02/267401.htm.
2 Patrick Lencioni, *The Advantage* (San Francisco: Jossey-Bass, 2012), http://www.azquotes.com/quote/740332.

Chapter 24

1 Neil Rackham, *Spin Selling* (New York: McGraw-Hill, 1988), 2.

Chapter 28

1 "92% of Millennials Believe That Success in Business Should Be Measured by More Than Profit (Deloitte, 2012)," Georgetown University, January 1, 2012, https://berkleycenter.georgetown.edu/quotes/92-of-millennials-believe-that-success-in-business-should-be-measured-by-more-than-profit-deloitte-2012.
2 "Burgum on Business: 9 Questions from FM business leaders," *Fargo Inc!*, October 3, 2016, http://www.fargoinc.com/burgum-on-business/.

Chapter 29

1 http://pastorrick.com/devotional/english/be-thankful-even-in-these-tough-times.

Chapter 30

1 Sigal Barsade and Olivia A. O'Neill, "Employees Who Feel Love Perform Better," *Harvard Business Review*, January 13, 2014, https://hbr.org/2014/01/employees-who-feel-love-perform-better.

2 Ken Blanchard and Phil Hodges, *Lead Like Jesus* (Nashville: Thomas Nelson, 2008), 29.

3 "You Never Know," *Ziglar*, May 29, 2015, https://www.ziglar.com/quotes/you-never-know/.

Appendix: The Five Capitals

1 Copyright 2017 Five Capitals, brandon@fivecapitals.net.

2 Copyright 2017 Five Capitals, brandon@fivecapitals.net.

☼ Acknowledgments

They say it takes a village to raise a child. I say that it takes a village to write a book. My heartfelt gratitude to every one of the following.

My husband, friend, and business partner, Gordon, who's a constant source of encouragement and insight ... and laughter.

My children and their spouses (although Danae isn't married yet), whom I truly love and respect. I'm so proud of all of them. Plus, they are always willing to "correct" my thinking and provide me insightful, instructive feedback on alternative perspectives.

Mentors, which are too many to name! A client of mine, David Ringenberger, president of Protection System, LLC, recently said, "A couple of years ago, when young entrepreneurs would ask me how I had built such a successful business, I'd talk about my drive, my creative ideas, and a long list of things I had done. However, now when they ask me the question, I respond very differently. As I reflect on my life, I tell them at key points in time, a key mentor or coach appeared. I did not intentionally seek them. They were just there. That perspective has changed my approach to business. I am always on the lookout for people from whom I am supposed to learn an important lesson. Or, vice versa, someone whom I am supposed to encourage and help."

As I consider my own life, that's what's happened to me too. It's overwhelmingly humbling to see all the leaders who have challenged and strengthened me along my leadership and spiritual journeys. I'm humbled by God's abundant provision and guidance. I hope that I can live up to their legacy. The following are the first few mentors and coaches on my long list.

Church youth group leader Jud Boyd, who supported me to

keep developing my leadership skills, even though I was petrified at the time and felt like an underdog.

My first manager at Xerox, Bob Klein, for always believing that a premed student could be successful in cold calling and capital equipment sales.

Mary Philipsek, Xerox manager (currently channel executive at Apple), for continually exemplifying sales leadership mastery and a thirst for excellence.

Larry Kutzler, City Sites, for embracing my entrepreneurial ideas and encouraging me to exercise and strengthen my voice via media.

Priscilla Mohrenweiser, *Letters from the King* contributor, for faithfully reminding me that in the midst of all life's turmoil, it's about love.

Jill Konrath, founder of Women Sales Pros and author of *More Sales, Less Time*, for relentlessly daring me to pursue my passions and my calling.

Marge Johnson, a discipler of women, for nurturing me to be a Proverbs 31 woman who steadfastly seeks to be God's best at home and work.

Floyd Adelman, CEO peer group chair, for trusting me enough to advise me to build a vibrant sales development firm.

Greg Meland, whom I worked with while he was Director of Supervised Ministry & Placement at Bethel University, for encouraging me to wrestle with God's call on my life and introducing me to the book *Let Your Life Speak: Listening for the Life of Vocation*. All who work with him at his current role as Director of Spiritual and Vocational Development at United Theological Seminary of the Twin Cities are in wise hands.

David Monroy, attorney and work-faith-integration practitioner, for collaborating and providing strategic wisdom and insight on reaching the next generation leaders.

If you are reading this list and wondering why your name is

not on the list, it probably is on my long list. You get the picture. Thank you for giving of yourself.

Millennials reviewers. Thirteen millennials, whom I have tremendous respect for, took the time to review portions of the manuscript and provide straightforward feedback, recommendations, and suggestions. I'm humbled that they gave time out of their crazy-busy schedules to invest the time to reflect and respond so authentically.

Coaches, prayer team, and friends. There were numerous times I reached out, crying, "Help!" Every time, they respond with thoughtful, powerful prayers. I'm humbled by their willingness to join this effort of raising up leaders of character to serve our world.

Clients. Sometimes I think, *I must be the luckiest person in the whole world! How could I get the best clients in the whole world?* They are incredible people of character whom I'm always learning from.

Virtual assistants. I have a team in South Africa who supports my efforts. I would not have been able to accomplish this work without their support and creative input.

Editors. This project would not have happened without awesome editors who supported me along the way.

Parents and siblings. I have learned much from each of you. I am grateful for your gifts, talents, insights, and perspectives, and I trust that we will continue to work together to show hospitality to those in our pathways.

About the Author

Danita Bye is founder and CEO of Sales Growth Specialists, a leadership and sales development firm that collaborates with business owners to improve sales performance as part of their growth strategy. She is also a member of Forbes Coaches Council.

Danita gained valuable experience at Xerox Corporation in various sales roles in the capital equipment and high tech world. Then she was an equity partner of a medical device company and had the responsibility of building and growing the sales team. She excelled as a salesperson, but her greatest success was her ability to find and mentor young talent. Danita saw firsthand how character-based leadership positively impacts both the company bottom line as well as the young professionals she coached.

With a practical, rubber-meets-the-road style, Danita strives to be a catalyst for experienced business leaders who are open to understanding the importance of their role in shaping young leaders. Her vision is to energize and equip leaders of character with the skills and tools to mentor millennials, our future leaders. She believes that the key responsibility of leaders is to build leaders.

Danita grew up on an isolated cattle ranch in rural North Dakota where she had strong mentors at home, church, and school. During those formative years, she learned about the value of money, relationships, discipline, education, and faith. Danita's leadership drive and sales management successes are rooted in her invaluable experiences on the ranch.

Millennials Matter is a culmination of principles gathered during Danita's years in sales and coaching. These principles are integrated with her spiritual passion. She has also authored *Letters from the King: A Devotional Parable of Spiritual Discovery* and *How to Hire Superior Sales DNA*. Danita writes a leadership blog at DanitaBye.com, which provides tips, tools, and talk tracks for those who mentor emerging leaders.

Committed to the development of the next generation of leaders, she has served on the board of trustees for two private Christian universities. In addition, she serves on the North Dakota Economic Development Foundation and North Dakota Petroleum Council.

She holds a master's degree in Transformational Leadership from Bethel University and a bachelor's degree in Premed and Psychology from the University of Sioux Falls.

Danita and her husband, Gordon, have been married for more than thirty years. After living for most of their married life in Minneapolis, they recently relocated back to the valley, the home of The Triple T in Stanley, North Dakota. They have three millennial children, Brittany, Westin, and Danae, and are the proud grandparents of two active boys. Danita enjoys traveling to Minneapolis and spending time with her family, reading, hiking, having coffee with friends, and traveling the globe in search of new friends and good coffee in places such as China, Tanzania, France, and Panama.

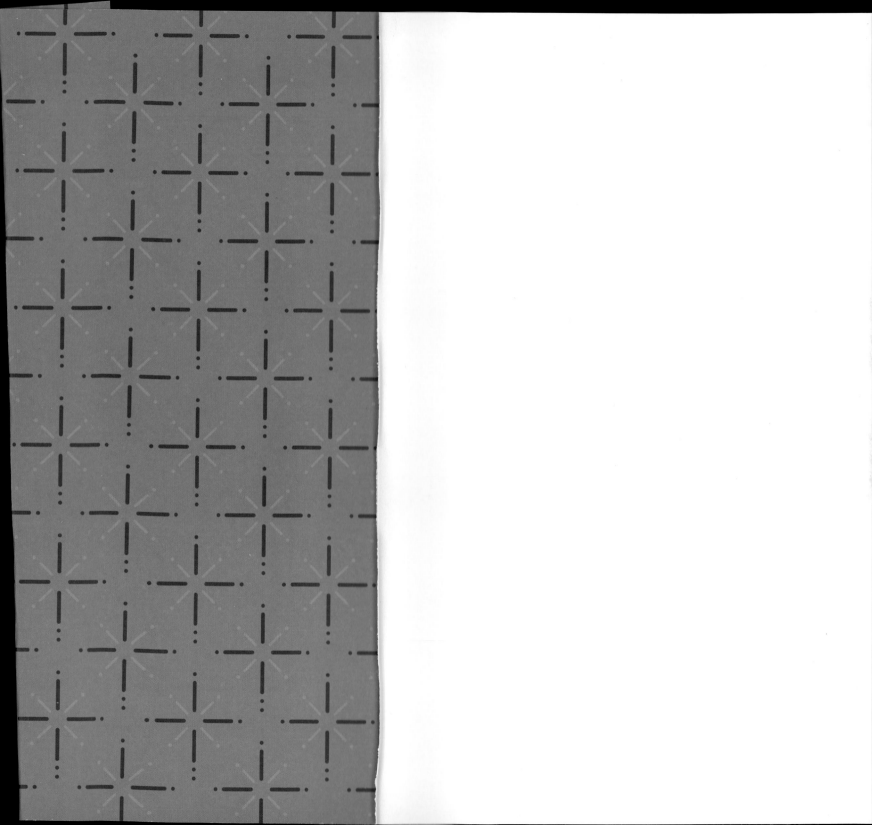

DanitaBye.com

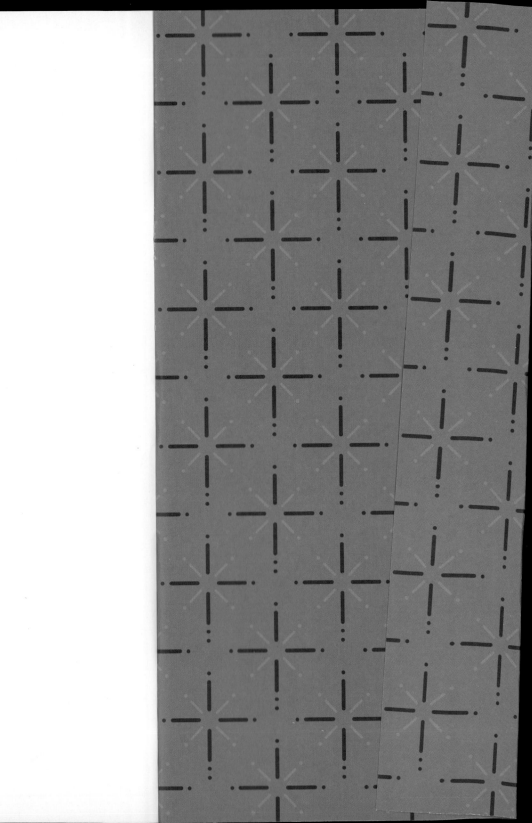